PETER G.L. HAMMOND.

A Guide to the
Family Law (Scotland) Act 1985

H.R.M. Macdonald

CCH Editions Limited

TAX, BUSINESS AND LAW PUBLISHERS

Published by CCH Editions Limited
Telford Road, Bicester, Oxfordshire OX6 0XD
Tel. (0869)253300, Facsimile (0869)245814.
USA   Commerce Clearing House Inc., Chicago, Illinois.
CANADA   CCH Canadian Limited, Toronto, Ontario.
AUSTRALIA   CCH Australia Limited, North Ryde, NSW.
NEW ZEALAND   Commerce Clearing House (NZ), Auckland.

About the Publisher

CCH Editions Limited is the United Kingdom affiliate of Commerce Clearing House Inc., a publishing company which provides leading tax and business law reporting services in the United States.

Other affiliates in Australia, Canada and New Zealand provide similar authoritative services in those countries.

A highly qualified editorial staff and many years of experience stand behind all CCH publications.

Disclaimer

This publication is designed to provide accurate and authoritative information in regard to the subject matter covered. It is sold with the understanding that the publisher is not engaged in rendering legal or other professional services. If legal advice or other expert assistance is required, the services of a competent professional person should be sought.

Ownership of Trade Marks

The Trade Marks

COMPUTAX and **COMMERCE, CLEARING, HOUSE,, INC.,** are the

property of Commerce Clearing House Incorporated, Chicago, Illinois, U.S.A.

First published 1986
Reprinted 1987
ISBN 0 86325 080 7

Typeset and printed in the United Kingdom by CCH Editions Limited.

Preface

The purpose of this book is to explain the fundamental changes to the law of Scotland made by the Family Law (Scotland) Act 1985. The principal changes are on financial provision on divorce and in the categories of those who owe obligations of financial support.

The Act, except for s. 25, comes into force on 1 September 1986. (It is understood that s. 25 will be brought into force when the law on diligence is reformed.) There are some retrospective provisions, but in general the Act applies only to actions raised on or after 1 September 1986.

It is hoped that this book will provide a guide which will be of assistance both to practitioners and to students.

Professor Robert Black, Professor of Scots Law in the University of Edinburgh, kindly read the manuscript and suggested many valuable amendments which are gratefully acknowledged. He is not, however, responsible for any expressions of opinion contained in the book, which are those of the author alone.

The Act is closely modelled upon recommendations made by the Scottish Law Commission, which were accepted with very minor modifications by Parliament. The author wishes to make clear that any expressions of opinion contained in the book do not in any way commit the Scottish Law Commission or the Scottish Office (which is the Government department responsible for this area of the law of Scotland).

H.R.M. Macdonald
September 1986

About the Author

Hugh Macdonald is an advocate. Previously he was a solicitor, and was for 14 years a member of the legal staff of the Scottish Law Commission. He was closely involved in much of the Commission's work in the field of family law, including the preparation of the reports implemented by the Family Law (Scotland) Act 1985.

Contents

Contents

1 Introduction

General

The Family Law (Scotland) Act 1985 (referred to throughout this book as 'the Act', 'the 1985 Act' or some similar phrase) makes fundamental changes to the Scots law of aliment – that is, obligations of financial support between husband and wife and between near relatives – and to the law of financial provision on divorce. It also makes minor changes to the law on the property of married couples. The Act is rather longer than practitioners will be accustomed to in the field of family law; nevertheless, the author does not believe that, by modern legislative standards, the Act is particularly complex. Indeed, the most striking innovations – the new principles governing financial provision on divorce – are drafted in the closest approximation to plain English which United Kingdom legislation can achieve. What complexities there are chiefly lie in the numerous cross-references, without which the Act would have been much longer. This book attempts to provide a straightforward guide to the Act's provisions and to their implications.

Background to the Act

In common with almost all other western countries Scotland has in recent years experienced an upsurge in the rate of divorce. It appears that between a quarter and a third of all marriages may be expected to end in divorce. The social and economic implications of this trend – particularly the effect on children – are not fully understood (though valuable research work has been carried out by the Central Research Unit of the Scottish Office – see *The Nature and Scale of Aliment and Financial Provision on Divorce* by Barbara Doig (1982); and *Children in Divorce* by Susan Seale (1984); and by Ann Mitchell in *Children in the Middle* (1985)). The Finer Committee (see Report of the Committee on One-Parent Families, 1974 Cmnd 5629) made clear that the financial position of one-parent families, particularly fatherless families, can be extremely vulnerable. The Act recognizes that the presence of dependent children in a family is an important factor in relation to financial provision on divorce, but it does not purport to offer a solution to an intractable problem. As

1

the Finer Committee put it, the law cannot extract 'more than a pint from a pint pot' (para. 4.59). The improvement of the general living conditions of divorced persons and their children cannot be achieved by reforming the principles of private law. In England and Wales, the courts are now directed to give the 'first consideration' to the welfare of children (Matrimonial and Family Proceedings Act 1984, s. 3). No such clarion call appears in the new Scottish legislation. Many of the new substantive rules do, nevertheless, concentrate on the needs of children: notably the right of a mother to apply for financial provision for herself until the youngest child of the marriage is sixteen (s. 9 (1) (c)); and the power of the court to give the mother and children the right to occupy the matrimonial home (s. 14 (2) (d)). Moreover, the Act preserves the general right of young children to be alimented by their parents. The Act does not, however, seek to accelerate the succession rights of children, on the view that these rights do not depend on the marital status of the parents.

In recent years a number of criticisms were levelled at the previous law on financial provision. The principal criticism was that too much depended upon the discretion of the judge. Uniformity of approach was not achieved even when the Court of Session had exclusive jurisdiction to hear actions of divorce – in particular, judicial attitudes varied on the relevance of marital misconduct. There was much resentment among divorced husbands (and their subsequent partners) where a wife was awarded long-term maintenance, especially where the marriage had been short and the wife's earning capacity had not been significantly impaired. This problem was exacerbated by the decision of the First Division of the Court of Session in *Chalmers* v *Chalmers* 1983 SLT 535, that the court had no power to award a periodical allowance for a fixed period (rather than until the wife's death or remarriage). Whatever virtues a system of unfettered judicial discretion may be supposed to have had, it became clear that uniformity of approach would be quite impossible to achieve once the sheriff courts were given jurisdiction in divorce actions.

The new Act is closely modelled upon recommendations made by the Scottish Law Commission, mainly in its Report on Aliment and Financial Provision (Scot. Law Com. No. 67, November 1981). Indeed, many of the changes made to the draft Bill appended to the Commission's Report were the subject of discussion between Government officials and representatives of the Commission closely involved in the subject matter. The Commission, as is its custom, had published a comprehensive consultative memorandum on aliment and financial provision in March 1976 (No. 22), which was widely circulated. Work commenced on the preparation of a Report in 1980, and as the scheme on financial provision evolved it was discussed with a large number of experienced practitioners. The scheme in the Report (and in the Act) might appear to some to be controversial – any proposals in this area of law can hardly avoid being controversial in certain respects – but it received the support of the professional legal bodies and of a wide range of organisations representing those most closely affected by divorce. Many of the subsequent criticisms of the Act, indeed, concern matters which are omitted from the legislation and which the Commission's Report did not cover: such as the plight of one-parent families, the difficulty in enforcing maintenance awards, the need for improved conciliation facilities and the perceived need for 'family courts'.

Scope of the Act

The opening sections of the Act (ss. 1–7) simplify and restate in statutory form the elements of the law of aliment, which hitherto has been almost entirely regulated by the common law. The most significant change is to abolish the obligation of a child to support his parents, and to terminate the parental obligation of support when the child reaches the age of eighteen (or, where he is receiving further education, a maximum age of twenty five). These changes are, however, unlikely to make much difference in practice – legal claims by parents or by adult children are extremely rare and, at least in the latter case, are viewed with suspicion by the courts.

Sections 8 to 16 remove the unfettered judicial discretion to award financial provision on divorce and substitute a new scheme, which depends partly on fixed principles (or heads of claim) and partly on the exercise of judicial discretion. Perhaps the most notable feature is the introduction of the concept of matrimonial property – in effect, what is acquired by the joint efforts or income of husband and wife during the effective period of the marriage – and the general rule that such property should be divided equally between husband and wife on divorce. There is no place in the new scheme for the previous practice of awarding to a wife perhaps a third of her husband's total assets – including property he owned before the marriage or inherited during the marriage. The scheme as a whole will prevent the arbitrary award of a long-term periodical allowance where this is not justified by the circumstances – indeed, there are provisions calculated to discourage awards in the form of a periodical allowance whenever another method – such as the transfer of property, or the payment of a capital sum by instalments – is available.

Another important feature is the rule on conduct. The provision of new principles (or heads of claim) enables conduct to be dealt with in different ways depending on the particular ground(s) of claim. Conduct is henceforth irrelevant (unless it has affected the economic basis of the claim) where a wife is claiming what she has 'earned' during the marriage – notably her share of the value of the matrimonial property. Where, however, she needs long-term maintenance the court can take her conduct into account, but only if it would be manifestly inequitable to leave it out of account.

The new scheme on financial provision on divorce applies also to actions of declarator of nullity (s. 17). Until the commencement of the Act the court's powers in nullity actions were restricted to ordering the restitution of property.

There follow a number of supplemental provisions in ss. 18–23, most of which are common to both aliment and financial provision, such as increased powers of the court to counteract avoidance transactions and – for the first time – a judicial power to order parties to provide details of financial resources.

Finally, there are provisions in ss. 24–26 which make minor changes to the law on the property of married couples. These implement another Report of the Scottish Law Commission (Report on Matrimonial Property, Scot. Law Com. No. 86, March 1984).

Relationship with Other Parts of the United Kingdom

Practitioners will be familiar with the type of difficulty which can arise when one or other of the parties crosses the Border. Apart from making appropriate amendments to the Maintenance Orders Act 1950, the new Act does not address itself to these difficulties. In future, the anomalies which can arise – depending, for example, on which country's courts have jurisdiction – will if anything be more marked than before. However, the reader should not assume too readily that the fault lies in the new Scottish legislation. A few illustrations will suffice, the first two of which are based on problems brought to the attention of the Scottish Law Commission during the course of its work.

Illustration 1

Mr and Mrs Murdoch and their son lived in Dumfries. They were all domiciled in Scotland. They separated, and Mr Murdoch moved to Carlisle. Mrs Murdoch subsequently raised a divorce action in Scotland (under rules of jurisdiction which apply to both countries – Divorce and Matrimonial Proceedings Act 1973, ss. 5 and 7). The court *inter alia* awarded aliment for Master Murdoch until he reached the age of sixteen. After reaching the age of eighteen he wished to obtain further aliment from his father to enable him to complete his education. Unfortunately, his father has now acquired an English domicile and, the English law of maintenance being remedy-based, his son has no independent right to seek maintenance from his father in the English courts. Moreover, it is too late for his mother to seek further aliment on his behalf in the Scottish divorce action.

Illustration 2

Mr and Mrs Stevens lived in Portsmouth. They were both domiciled in England. They were divorced there, and Mrs Stevens obtained an order for a periodical allowance. Mr Stevens subsequently moved to Glasgow, and died there some years later after acquiring a Scottish domicile. Unfortunately for Mrs Stevens, the English order automatically ceased on Mr Stevens' death (Matrimonial Causes Act 1973, s. 28 (1)), and Mrs Stevens has succession rights neither under English law (the right to apply for a discretionary payment out of the deceased's estate being available only when he died domiciled in England and Wales: Inheritance (Provision for Family and Dependants) Act 1975, s. 1 (1)) nor under Scots law (the Succession (Scotland) Act 1964 confers no rights of succession on divorced persons). Had she been receiving a periodical allowance from a Scottish court, it would not automatically have ceased on Mr Stevens' death (s. 13).

Illustration 3

Mr Maxwell is retired and lives in Perthshire. He is domiciled in Scotland, and is very, very rich. He marries a chorus girl. She has no money of her own. They part very soon after the marriage. She decides to pick up the threads of her career and, because of the financial climate, has to seek work in England. After the required residence period in England (minimum: one year) she raises divorce proceedings there. A beneficent judge awards her one-third of her husband's total assets, all of which were acquired before his marriage. Had the divorce action been raised in Scotland, she would have received little or nothing under ss. 8 and 9 of the Act.

2 Obligations of Aliment

Parties to the Obligation

1. Introduction

The Act considerably reduces the categories of alimentary obligants. As from the commencement of the Act obligations of aliment are owed by a husband to his wife; a wife to her husband; a parent to a child, subject to age limits (see p. 8); and a person to a child whom he has accepted as a child of his family (see p. 9). There are no other obligations of aliment. However, the Act makes no change in the rule that, in certain circumstances, there may be an equitable claim against the estate of a deceased relative or against those enriched by the succession to the estate of a relative. This rule is expressly preserved by s. 1 (4). (There are many ambiguities and uncertainties in this rule, which the Scottish Law Commission proposes to examine in the course of its forthcoming review of the law of succession.)

2. Husband and wife

At common law a husband was bound to aliment his wife. A wife's liability towards her husband was regulated by statute, but in language which suggested that there might be no obligation if the husband could maintain himself at subsistence level (Married Women's Property (Scotland) Act 1920, s. 4). The Act removes this distinction and imposes fully reciprocal obligations of aliment on spouses. This principle applies also to the parties to a polygamous marriage, provided that the marriage is regarded as valid by Scots law (s. 1 (5)). Previously, parties to a polygamous marriage could raise actions for aliment (Matrimonial Proceedings (Polygamous Marriages) Act 1972, s. 2) but, in the absence of a decree, there was doubt about a right to aliment *ex lege*.

3. Parent and child

At common law there was a reciprocal obligation between parent and legitimate child, during the lifetime of either. By statute, an adopted child and adoptive parent were placed in the same position. The Adoption (Scotland) Act 1978, s. 39 (1) treats an adopted child in law as if he were born as a legitimate child of the marriage (or, as the case may be, the adopter) and as if he were not the child of any other person. Both parents were bound to support an illegitimate child, but not vice versa (*Clarke* v *Carfin Coal Co.* (1891) 18 R (HL) 63). There was a limited remedy-based discretionary power enabling a court hearing an action of divorce, nullity of marriage or separation to make an order providing for the maintenance of a child who was the child of one party to the marriage (including an illegitimate child) and who had been accepted as one of the family by the other party (Matrimonial Proceedings (Children) Act 1958, s. 7 (1)). Such a child was not obliged to support the 'accepting parent'. But otherwise there was no alimentary obligation between step-parent and step-child.

The principal change in the Act is to remove the liability of any child to support either of his parents. This has the effect of placing legitimate, adopted and illegitimate children in exactly the same position.

The parental obligation is now more restricted than it was. Previously there was no age limit on a child's entitlement to aliment. The parent of a legitimate child (and an adopter) had a legal obligation to support the child, at least in theory, during their joint lives. The obligation on the parent of an illegitimate child may have been less open-ended. The obligation may only have lasted until the child became capable of earning his own livelihood. Moreover, it was suggested that an illegitimate child who had been self-supporting, and afterwards became indigent, had no legal right to aliment from his parents (*Clarke* v *Carfin Coal Co.* (1891) 18 R (HL) 63 per Lord Watson at pp. 68–9). The parents of an illegitimate child were also bound by statute to support him until a maximum age of twenty one (Affiliation Orders Act 1952, s. 3, now repealed) but this did not exclude the possibility of continuing parental liability at common law.

Both parents of a legitimate, illegitimate or adopted child are now liable to support him, but only until he reaches the age of eighteen; or, where he is 'reasonably and appropriately' undergoing instruction at an educational establishment, or training for employment or for a trade, profession or vocation, until he reaches the maximum age of twenty five (ss. 1 (1) (*c*), (*d*) and 1 (5)). The word 'employment' is used to make clear that the extension up to the age of twenty five is not confined to one of the traditionally recognized trades or professions. The instruction or training need not be full-time. A student could sue his parents if they failed to pay the contribution expected of them under the students' grants scheme. The phrase 'reasonably and appropriately' merely mirrors the existing equitable approach of the common law. The broad question is to determine when a child can reasonably be regarded as ceasing to be a dependant of his parents. No further guidance is offered by the Act as to what is reasonable and appropriate. The court will have regard to whether the education is appropriate to the child's needs and ability and, where relevant, to the resources available to the parent. If a parent argues that his child was unnecessarily prolonging his period of dependence, for example by taking a second degree at a university, much might depend on the field of study and on whether the acquisition of a second degree was essential or desirable for the student's future employment prospects.

4. 'Accepted' children

If a person has 'accepted' a child as a child of his family, he is liable to aliment him until he reaches the age of eighteen or twenty five (in the same way as described at p. 8 above). Section 1 (1) (*d*) creates, for the first time, a direct alimentary relationship between 'parent' and child and replaces the remedy-based approach of the Matrimonial Proceedings (Children) Act 1958, s. 7 (1). The wording is wider than that of the 1958 Act. The child need not be the child of the other party to the marriage. Where there are two adults in the family, they need not be married to one another – indeed, they may be of the same sex. There need not, however, be another adult – a family includes a one-parent family (s. 27 (1), definition of 'family'). Thus, a bachelor uncle or a maiden aunt may 'accept' a single nephew or niece as a child of the family. The same concept was used in the Damages (Scotland) Act 1976 to describe one of the categories of relative entitled to sue for loss of support and loss of society (Sch. 1, para. 1 (*c*): '. . . accepted by the deceased as a child of his family'). There has been no reported judicial interpretation of the 1976 Act phrase. The effect of the new provision is that a man may be found liable to aliment the children of his cohabitant by a previous marriage or association. This does not necessarily mean that an 'accepting parent' will be found liable as a matter of course, or even more often than not. The natural parents of the child will also be liable, and it is unlikely that an 'accepting parent' will be ordered to pay aliment if either or both of the natural parents can support the child (see p. 12).

'Acceptance' connotes that the obligant personally regarded the child as a member of his family. The concept thus goes beyond a mere requirement that the child was *treated* as a member of the family, the phrase now used in English legislation (Matrimonial Causes Act 1973, s. 52 (1)) – which would require proof of purely objective facts and might lead to the unfair imposition of liability. More importantly, it connotes permanent membership of the family until forisfamiliation. The difference between the concepts of 'accepted' and 'treated' may be illustrated by the following examples. In the course of his employment a widower is posted abroad for a period of five years to a place with an inclement climate. He prefers that his children should remain in Scotland, and asks an old family friend to look after them until his return. The friend agrees. Five years later the widower returns and resumes the care of his children. The friend has not 'accepted' the children into his family in the sense envisaged by the Act, and no alimentary liability arises. If, however, a widower had died and a close family friend took over responsibility for his children, who were still

9

living with him by the time they left school, the friend would probably be held to have 'accepted' the children into his family.

In the absence of reported Scottish cases on the interpretation of the phrase, it is impossible to predict with confidence exactly when a person will be regarded as having 'accepted' a child into his family. There are English authorities on the terms 'accepted' and 'treated', some more helpful to a Scottish practitioner than others. There seems no reason why a child *in utero* could not be 'accepted' in suitable circumstances, for example if a man was living with and had undertaken to marry a woman who was carrying another man's child (on an application of the *nasciturus* principle: see e.g. *Caller* v *Caller* [1968] P 39). On the other hand, the mere fact that a man married a woman who already had children by a previous marriage would not by itself be enough to make him liable to aliment her children (see e.g. *Bowlas* v *Bowlas* [1965] P 450). Awkward questions may arise where a couple separate (see e.g. *B.* v *B. and F.* [1969] P 37). Much may depend on the length of the period of cohabitation. It seems unlikely that a Scottish court would follow *Snow* v *Snow* [1972] Fam 74, where a man was held liable for maintenance after a period of cohabitation of only four months.

A person does not accept a child, in the sense of incurring alimentary liability, if the child has been boarded out with him by a local or other public authority or a voluntary organisation (s. 1 (1) (*d*)). This exception is designed to protect, in particular, foster parents. Where a child is boarded out with foster parents by a local authority, the child technically remains in the care of the local authority and the arrangement with the foster parents is to some extent a temporary and commercial one. The exception in s. 1 (1) (*d*), by referring to a 'public authority', extends to arrangements made by the appropriate authorities for the care of children of British subjects serving abroad in an official capacity. The position may be different where the arrangement is a purely private one between a parent and a foster parent which does not involve a local authority or voluntary organisation. The expressions local authority and public authority are not defined, nor were they defined in the corresponding English legislation (Matrimonial Causes Act 1973, s. 52 (1)). 'Voluntary organisation' is defined by s. 27 (1) to mean a body the activities of which are not carried on for profit.

5.   No other obligations of aliment

The obligations described above are the only surviving legal obligations of aliment. Under the previous law there was no alimentary obligation between collaterals (such as brothers and sisters), between relations by affinity, or between the parents of an illegitimate child, and none is created by the Act (but see the discussion at p. 23 on the meaning of 'inlying expenses' in s. 3 (1) (*b*)). Any reciprocal alimentary obligations between grandparent and grandchild are abolished. These obligations under the previous law only came into being (a) in the legitimate line and (b) where the intermediate generation could not provide support. Where any obligation is abolished, it ceases to have effect as from the commencement of the Act. Any decree against a person whose liability ceases to exist at that date automatically ceases to have effect (s. 1 (3)). Any arrears due under the decree are, however, recoverable (s. 1 (4)).

When Liability Arises

1. Introduction

Generally speaking, the new legislation does not lay down specific conditions as to when liability will or will not arise. Instead it refers to a number of factors, some or all of which will be relevant in considering whether a particular person is, in the circumstances, liable to pay aliment and if so how much. One partial exception to this is conduct – the conduct of a party, especially a wife, may in certain circumstances disentitle her to aliment, irrespective of her needs and her husband's resources (s. 4 (3) (*b*)). This question is discussed below (see p. 25; p. 49). The various factors identified in the Act include the needs and resources of the parties and the existence of other potential alimentary debtors. These are discussed in Chapter 3. Cases where there is more than one debtor and where there is more than one creditor are considered below.

2. Order of liability

The Act abolishes any rules of the common law whereby one person has a primary responsibility to aliment a particular creditor (s. 4 (2)). The main effect is to abolish the rule of the common law that the father of a legitimate child has the primary liability for his support. The mother's liability arose only where the father was unable to provide support. In future both parents will in principle be equally liable, subject always to modification in the light of each parent's resources. This brings the general law into line with the existing rule on the liability of the parents of illegitimate children.

This change will not make any practical difference in a great many cases, notably where a separated or divorced mother has care of the children of the marriage and is unable to work. It will, however, make a significant difference, as between the parents, where both are able to work and especially where their earning capacity is similar (or indeed where the mother's means are greater). In certain circumstances the effect of the new rule will be that a father will incur no liability at all to his children. An illustration is provided by the circumstances in *Galt* v *Turner* 1981 SLT (Notes)' 99, where a man of limited earning capacity had remarried and reversed traditional roles with his second wife, who went out to work to support the family. It

11

seems inconceivable that an action at the instance of his first wife, claiming periodical allowance for herself and aliment for the children of the first marriage, could succeed under the principles of the new Act. (Whether these principles will influence the attitude of the court where, as in *Galt* v *Turner*, a father is prosecuted under the Supplementary Benefits Act 1976, s. 25 (1), for persistently refusing and neglecting to maintain the children of his first marriage, is a matter for speculation.)

Where the obligants include both a natural parent and an 'accepting parent', the Act does not stipulate who is principally liable. A rigid rule is no more necessary than in the case of father and mother. The most common case will be where a man has accepted his wife's children by a previous marriage and subsequently separates from her. As under the previous law (Matrimonial Proceedings (Children) Act 1958, s. 7 (2), now repealed), the court will be able to take into account the liability of the natural parents. The question will often be resolved by a consideration of the overall current responsibilities of the parties. If, for example, the 'accepting parent' has set up a new household and acquired new financial responsibilities, the court can take this into account, whether or not he owes a legal obligation of aliment to any member of the new household (s. 4 (3) (*a*)). If the mother and her children have become members of a new household, she and her children may be supported by someone else. Much may depend on whether any of the parties are in receipt of social security. It should be noted that 'accepting parents' are not liable relatives for supplementary benefit purposes (Supplementary Benefits Act 1976, s. 17).

The common law provided that a person's relatives were liable to aliment him in a certain order (spouse, descendants, father, mother, etc.). The only obligants now will be spouse and parents. The restriction on the categories of obligant makes it unnecessary to retain the common law hierarchy or even to simplify it in the light of the new law. Where two or more persons are liable, the court, in deciding how much aliment (if any) to award against any of them, is to have regard *inter alia* to the liability of the other obligant(s) (s. 4 (2)). Thus if a married student aged eighteen claimed aliment from his father, rather than from his working wife, his father would be theoretically liable, but the court would take into account all the circumstances, including his wife's liability.

3. Order of entitlement

The Act does not lay down any particular order of entitlement to aliment from a single alimentary debtor. The problem is of very slight importance in view of the restriction on the categories of obligant. The only claimants will be spouse and children of various kinds. Thus, if a person is sued both by his separated wife and by his student son, the court would take into account all the circumstances, including the existence of both claims and a single set of resources on the part of the debtor.

4. Reimbursement of aliment

The Act contains no rules on reimbursement of aliment. The existing law, which is not affected, depends on common law principles of unjustified enrichment. A person will often be presumed to make a donation, by virtue of close relationship, and will therefore be unable to claim reimbursement. If, however, a shopkeeper supplies a wife with necessaries he may claim to be reimbursed by a husband who is failing to support her (see Clive, *Husband and Wife* (2nd edn), pp. 276–8). The abolition of the wife's *praepositura* by the Law Reform (Husband and Wife) (Scotland) Act 1984, s. 7, does not affect a husband's alimentary liability in these circumstances.

The Act also repeals (see Sch. 2) certain words in the Conjugal Rights (Scotland) Amendment Act 1861, s. 6, which stated that a husband was not liable for his separated wife's obligations. The repealed words were always unnecessary. In the first place, a separated wife had no *praepositura*; secondly, a husband might be liable on principles of unjustified enrichment (as just described) if he was not alimenting his wife.

5. Termination of obligation

An obligation of aliment ends with the end of the alimentary relationship. Thus, on divorce there is no longer an obligation of aliment between husband and wife. (This, of course, is without prejudice to the right of either party to seek financial provision on divorce – see Chapters 4 and 5.) The obligation to a child ceases automatically when the child reaches the age of eighteen or, if undergoing further education, twenty five (s. 1 (5)). An obligation of aliment is owed only by parties falling within the categories mentioned in s. 1, and an obligation abolished by the Act ceases to have effect on the commencement of the Act.

3 Actions for Aliment

Introduction

The Act contains a single set of provisions governing claims for aliment. The expression 'action for aliment' (see s. 2 (1), (2) and (3)) means:

- a claim for aliment alone;
- a claim in proceedings for divorce, separation, declarator of marriage or declarator of nullity of marriage;
- a claim in proceedings relating to orders for financial provision;
- a claim in proceedings concerning rights and obligations in relation to children, or parentage or legitimacy; or
- a claim in proceedings of any other kind, where the court considers it appropriate to include a claim for aliment.

This last category affords some discretion to the court to deal in one action with matters at issue between the parties to a matrimonial dispute. Separate rules, however, apply to interim aliment *pendente lite* (i.e. pending disposal of the action) (see p. 28), and the discussion which follows does not apply to such claims. An action for aliment as described above is competent both in the Court of Session and in the sheriff court (s. 2 (1)). Section 2 does not extend the jurisdiction of the sheriff so as to entertain actions of declarator of marriage or of nullity of marriage.

The Act abolishes a number of *ad hoc* statutory rules of jurisdiction, and at the same time sweeps away a series of incongruities and inconsistencies in the old law. Previously there was a number of express statutory provisions which are repealed by Sch. 2. In particular, the distinction between 'interim aliment' and 'permanent aliment' is abandoned. The expression 'interim aliment' is used in the Act solely to mean aliment *pendente lite*. The description of the rules of jurisdiction in the Sheriff Courts (Scotland) Act 1907 is also simplified by Sch. 1, para. 1. Apart from the provisions in s. 2 of the new Act, just described, s. 5 of the 1907 Act now confers (or restates) jurisdiction on the sheriff in actions for aliment or separation and for regulating the custody of children; actions arising out of an application under the Maintenance Orders (Reciprocal Enforcement) Act 1972, s. 3 (1) for the recovery of maintenance; and actions for divorce (s. 5 (2), (2A) and (2B)). The sheriff now has jurisdiction in an action for separation in which there is no conclusion for aliment.

In general the provisions on actions for aliment apply only to actions brought after the commencement of the Act. The provisions on variation and recall of decrees, however, apply to all applications made after the commencement date, even where the action was raised and the decree was granted under the previous law. There is also an element of retrospection in the provision on expenses of litigation (s. 22 (*c*); see p. 62) and in the provision on agreements (s. 7 (5); see p. 57).

Title to Sue

1.   General

Section 2 (4) simplifies the previous complex rules on title to sue in actions for aliment. The following can now sue:

(a)   a person to whom an obligation of aliment is owed, including a child;
(b)   the curator bonis of an incapax or the curator of a minor who is an incapax; and
(c)   on behalf of a child under the age of eighteen years:
   - the father or mother;
   - the tutor of a pupil; and
   - a person entitled to, seeking or having custody or care of the child.

Where a claim is made on behalf of a child, the true creditor is the child and not the person who actually makes the claim (see e.g. *Bell* v *McCurdie* 1981 SLT 159). The true creditor is, however, given a personal right to sue in every case. A 'child' in context includes an illegitimate child. The term 'child' is not, in context, subject to any age qualification apart from the age limits of eighteen (or twenty five) which mark the termination of the alimentary obligation. In practice, if a child is below the age of majority (eighteen), the action will usually be raised by someone else on his behalf. Thus a claim on behalf of a pupil child will be made by his tutor, who will generally be a parent. The separate reference to the mother of the child in s. 2 (4) (*c*) supersedes the common law rule that the mother of an illegitimate pupil child could sue for aliment even though she was not the child's tutrix.

Once a child reaches the age of eighteen it is inappropriate for a claim to be made on his behalf by someone else, and he must raise independent proceedings. Under the previous law a claim could not be made on behalf of a child after he reached the age of sixteen. This change will probably not have a marked effect on the practice of the courts in divorce actions. It does not mean, for example, that all awards of aliment

16

for children in actions for divorce will be made expressly to last until the child is eighteen. The normal practice will probably be to award aliment until the child is sixteen, especially where the mother obtains an order for financial provision for herself under s. 9 (1) (*c*) based on the need to share the economic burden of caring for the child until he is sixteen. The Act does not specify whether the age limit applies at the date of raising the action or at the date of decree. The court will presumably not grant decree if, at the latter date, the child is already eighteen.

Title to sue on behalf of a child is not confined to persons who have legal custody. Thus a grandparent who is bringing up a grandchild but did not wish to claim legal custody would have a title to sue; so would a tutor appointed by a deceased parent to act for a child who was in the care of someone else or who was being cared for in an institution. More generally, a court will not be obliged unnecessarily to determine questions of legal custody, when the real issue between the child's parents is liability for aliment. Both parents will continue to have joint legal custody in the absence of a court order depriving one of them of custody (Guardianship Act 1973, s. 10). Where they are agreed that they should continue to have equal parental rights there will be no need for the court to interfere, merely because it is being asked to determine the question of aliment.

Section 2 (4) (*c*) uses the words 'on behalf of' a child. This makes clear that the true creditor is the child and not the person who may be bringing the action. There will therefore be no risk of too much aliment being awarded simply because more than one person has a title to sue the debtor in respect of the same obligation of aliment. Similarly there will be no difficulty in obtaining a decree in a form which enables the aliment to be treated as the child's for income tax purposes. This was already possible under the previous law (*Mackay* v *Mackay* 1953 SLT (Notes) 69; *Huggins* v *Huggins* 1981 SLT 179: but see *Finnie* v *Finnie* 1984 SLT 109). The payee (even if he is not, for example, the tutor) can give a good receipt for aliment on behalf of the child (s. 2 (10)). There is no specific provision designed to ensure that the payee actually disburses the aliment on the child's behalf. (In *Smith* v *Smith*, 6 January 1984, unreported, Lord Stott terminated payments of aliment no longer being used for the maintenance of children by their mother, having regard to the definition of 'aliment' in *Bell's Dictionary*, 7th edn, p. 38: viz, maintenance, food, and clothing.) In many cases the payee will be subject to the law on tutors. If a divorced mother is adequately caring for her child, but is spending surplus aliment on luxuries for herself, the father can seek a reduction in the amount of aliment which he has been ordered to pay her by the court. Alternatively, he may in appropriate circumstances seek to enter into some arrangement whereby aliment is paid directly to a third party on the child's behalf, e.g. the payment of school fees directly to a school. In extreme cases he could, no doubt, have resort to the normal remedies for breach of trust.

Nothing in s. 2 (4) affects any right conferred by statute on any public or local authority to recover contributions from liable relatives in relation to children being supported out of public funds (Supplementary Benefits Act 1976, ss. 18 and 19; Social Work (Scotland) Act 1968, ss. 78–82).

Under the present law it seems clear that a curator bonis has a title to claim aliment for his ward (e.g. *Howard's Exor* v *Howard's Curator Bonis* (1894) 21 R 787; *Edinburgh Parish Council* v *Aitchison* (1919) 35 Sh Ct Rep 195). Section 2 (4) (*b*) restates this principle and also makes clear that the curator of a minor incapax has a title to sue for aliment for the minor. (No express provision is needed for a minor who is not incapax.) Section 2 (4) (*b*) does not define what is meant by a minor incapax, but the context makes clear that he is someone who is labouring under mental disability as well as lacking legal capacity. The Act does not deal with the question whether an action can be raised in the name of a mentally incapacitated person with a view to the appointment of a curator ad litem. This is probably not a problem of great practical importance and is in any event not confined to the law of aliment. (The procedure was allowed in the old case of *Pringle* v *Pringle* (1824) 3 S 248, but was criticized and disallowed in two other old cases: *Reid* v *Reid* (1839) 1 D 400; *Mackenzie* (1845) 7 D 283.) The approved modern procedure is for a curator bonis to be appointed and the alimentary action is then raised by him on behalf of the incapax.

2. Unborn children

Under the Illegitimate Children (Scotland) Act 1930, s. 3, an unmarried woman could raise an action of affiliation and aliment before the birth of a child. No proof was held and no decree granted until after the child's birth, except that if paternity was admitted or the action was undefended, the court could order a payment to account of inlying expenses and could grant decree for aliment to begin with the birth of the child. This was a useful procedure, because it enabled a mother to establish jurisdiction against a father who was likely to decamp and it enabled her to obtain aliment more quickly. The same problems can beset a married woman, and the Act therefore not only preserves the principle of the 1930 Act, but extends it to all women, whether married or not (s. 2 (5)). Several further qualifications in the 1930 Act provision have been omitted, notably that the mother-to-be should be six months pregnant before being allowed to raise an action. As a matter of evidence she would require to satisfy the court that she was pregnant. Accordingly the new provision is simply that a woman (whether married or not) may bring an action for aliment on behalf of her unborn child as if the child had been born, but no such action shall be heard or disposed of prior to the birth of the child. The power of the court to award inlying expenses is preserved (in s. 3 (1) (*b*)). The court will also be able to exercise its general power to award interim aliment *pendente lite* and to backdate awards (s. 3 (1) (*c*)) and these powers will be sufficient to cover the period before the action is disposed of.

Defences

1.   General

Various defences available under the common law are not affected by the Act – e.g. that there is no alimentary relationship, or that the respective needs and resources of the parties do not justify an award. Certain other aspects of the law are now dealt with specifically as defences.

2.   Cohabitation and support in the home

Under the previous law a woman could not sue for aliment for herself (or for her children) unless she was living apart from her husband. There was a limited statutory exception whereby the court could make an order for custody and aliment for a child under the Guardianship of Children (Scotland) Acts, but the order was not enforceable while the spouses resided together, and ceased to have effect if they continued so to reside for three months (Guardianship of Infants Act 1925, s. 3, as amended by Guardianship Act 1973, Sch. 4). This rule could cause hardship: a husband might be starving his wife and family of funds, and supplementary benefit is not normally available to a cohabiting wife (Supplementary Benefits Act 1976, Sch. 1).

The Act therefore provides, first, that it is competent to bring an action for aliment, notwithstanding that the person for or on behalf of whom aliment is being claimed is living in the same household as the defender; and, secondly, that it is to be a defence in these circumstances that the defender is fulfilling the obligation of aliment, and intends to continue doing so (s. 2 (6) and (7)). These two provisions are interlinked. It would be inappropriate to provide a general defence of this nature to a defender, separated from his wife, where his wife had raised proceedings in the reasonable belief that her husband was about to discontinue supporting her. In these circumstances she would be justified in wanting the comparative security of a decree in her favour. The provisions are not, needless to say, designed to encourage frivolous applications against husbands who are discharging their financial responsibilities to their families. Nonetheless, the onus of establishing the defence rests on the defender, but a pursuer will also require to establish facts indicating that she and her children are not being supported or that the defender is about to withhold support.

3.   Offer to provide support in the home: husband and wife

A further specific defence is that the defender is making an offer, which it is reasonable to expect the person on whose behalf aliment is being claimed to accept, to receive that person into his household and to fulfil the obligation of aliment. In considering whether it is reasonable to expect a person to accept an offer, the court is to have regard among other things to any conduct, decree or other circumstances which appear relevant: but the fact that a husband and wife have agreed to live apart shall not of itself be regarded as making it unreasonable to expect a person to accept such an offer (s. 2 (8) and (9)).

At first sight this may appear to be a novel defence, but it represents only a minor change in the existing law. For the sake of simplicity the following description assumes that the claimant is the wife. The underlying principle before 1977 was that a wife who was unwilling to live with her husband, without reasonable cause, was not entitled to claim aliment. A wife who was separated from her husband by consent could not obtain an award of aliment from him, except where he paid her voluntarily. A consensual separation was not regarded as reasonable cause for living apart. The underlying principle was preserved, with a minor modification, by the Divorce (Scotland) Act 1976 (s. 7 (1)). This enabled the court to award aliment if satisfied that:

'(a) the pursuer and the defender are not cohabiting with one another, and
(b) the pursuer is unwilling to cohabit with the defender whether or not the pursuer has reasonable cause for not so cohabiting by virtue of the circumstances set out in paragraph (a), (b) or (c) of section 1 (2) of this Act:

Provided that, where the pursuer does not have reasonable cause for not cohabiting as aforesaid, the court shall not grant decree if it is satisfied that the defender is willing to cohabit with the pursuer.'

The modification in many cases enabled a wife separated from her husband by consent to obtain an award of aliment. Her husband could still defeat the claim, however, by reneging on the agreement and satisfying the court that, after all, he was willing to live with her. The modification attempted to bring this branch of the law into line with the revised grounds of divorce introduced by the 1976 Act, notably the introduction of a ground based on mutual consent to divorce after two years' separation (s. 1 (2) (d)). In conformity with this main reform in the 1976 Act, a wife is regarded as having reasonable cause for not living with her husband if he has committed adultery, behaved unreasonably or deserted her.

Thus the post-1976 law concentrated on the conduct of the husband (defender) rather than on the conduct of the wife (pursuer). A wife who had committed adultery or behaved unreasonably towards her husband, as a result of which her husband had left her, was still entitled to aliment. If she had deserted him, however, she could not claim aliment if he offered to resume cohabitation. The law still permitted a husband to defeat his wife's claim to aliment, even where there had been a mutually agreed separation, provided he could satisfy the court that his offer to resume cohabitation was genuine and not just a device to evade financial liability. Perhaps the greatest single anomaly was between the law on aliment and the law on financial provision on divorce: a wife might be disentitled to aliment pending divorce but would normally, if she applied, receive a discretionary award of financial provision when decree of divorce was granted.

What s. 2 (8) and (9) of the new Act sets out to do is to abolish the rule that willingness to adhere is a condition of entitlement. As a principle of law the old approach was flawed. A wife who is unwilling to adhere, but has not yet left her husband, is entitled to aliment. So, strictly speaking, is a deserting wife – she is merely unable to recover aliment in money. She will be alimented in kind if she returns to her husband. The new provisions, phrased in terms of a defence, attempt to concentrate on the means of fulfilling an obligation of aliment. The onus is not on the wife to establish that her husband is not making a reasonable offer but on the husband to establish that he is.

The new provisions retain much of the flavour of the previous law. A husband can still renege on a consensual separation, because s. 2 (9) states that the fact that a husband and a wife have agreed to live apart shall not of itself be regarded as making it unreasonable to expect her to accept an offer. The reference to conduct in s. 2 (9) means that a wife will still be regarded as having reasonable excuse for not living with her husband if, for example, he has committed adultery or behaved unreasonably towards her. In addition there will be other circumstances in which an offer would not be regarded as reasonable: for example if either husband or wife had obtained a decree of judicial separation, or even perhaps if he was suffering from a disease or mental disorder which made it unreasonable to expect his wife to live with him.

Where the reason for separation is not a matrimonial offence such as adultery or unreasonable behaviour, the results of the new legislation are more difficult to predict. Until 1984 a husband was generally able to determine where the matrimonial home should be. Thus if a husband living in Dundee was offered a better-paid post in Aberdeen, his wife was generally obliged to follow him if she wanted to avoid giving him grounds for divorce for desertion. The husband's legal rights in this matter have now been removed by the Law Reform (Husband and Wife) (Scotland) Act 1984, s. 4. (The object of this Act was simply to abolish rules which discriminated against married women.) It is now open to the court to hold that either, or both, or neither party is in desertion, assuming that one of the parties chooses to sue on that ground. All that can be said with confidence is that a court would be precluded from holding that an offer was reasonable where the sole dispute between the parties concerned the place of the matrimonial home.

4. Offer to provide support in the home: parent and child

Under the previous law the parent of a legitimate (and probably also an illegitimate) child above the age of sixteen had a good defence to a claim for aliment if he offered to receive and support the child in his home, provided this would not be detrimental to the child's health (see e.g. *McKay* v *McKay* 1980 SLT (Sh Ct) 111). The defence contained in s. 2 (8) and (9) (see p. 19 above), is now available to the parent, although the question whether an offer is or is not reasonable will have to be judged against a

21

rather different background. It would presumably be unreasonable for a father living in Dundee to expect his student son to live at home while attending university in Glasgow. It would equally be unreasonable to expect a seventeen year old son to live at home if he was constantly subjected to physical assaults at the hands of his father. Each case will fall to be determined on its own merits.

The defence contained in s. 2 (8) and (9) does not apply where a child is under the age of sixteen. Any dispute over the residence of such a child would in practice be dealt with in custody proceedings before the question of aliment was decided.

Powers of the Court

1. General

The powers conferred on the court by the Act are more restricted in actions for aliment than in actions for divorce, although they are wider in several respects than before. The same powers are exercisable, with a single exception, in the Court of Session and in the sheriff court. The exception is the power to grant warrant for inhibition in terms of s. 19 (1) (see p. 60), which can only be exercised by the Court of Session. The court's powers are flexible and discretionary. There may, for example, be a number of reasons for refusing decree – such as a valid defence under s. 2, or the absence of need on the part of the claimant or of resources on the part of the obligant. In particular the court is not bound to award the full sum claimed (s. 3 (1) (*d*)). This represents the usual position at common law. The new general principle, however, extends also to actions of affiliation and aliment. Hitherto these were regarded as ordinary actions for debt: if the defender did not defend, the court was bound to grant decree for the full sum sued for.

2. Form of payments of aliment

The usual form of award is by way of periodical payments, and the Act simply restates the court's existing power (s. 3 (1) (*a*)). The decree may provide for aliment to be paid indefinitely or for a stipulated period – e.g. until the child attains the age of sixteen. The court has no power to substitute a lump sum for a periodical payment, and is expressly precluded from doing so by the new legislation (s. 3 (2)). The court is, however, given power to order the making of alimentary payments of an occasional or special nature, including payments in respect of inlying, funeral or educational expenses (s. 3 (1) (*b*)). The distinction is between a lump sum to meet a particular alimentary expense, and a lump sum which is a substitute for continuing liablity. The court can award the former but not the latter. Inlying and funeral expenses were already specified as recoverable under the Illegitimate Children (Scotland) Act 1930 (ss. 1 (2) and 5, now repealed).

Inlying expenses were not defined in the 1930 Act. In that context they have been described as covering the cost of such items as 'garments, toilet articles, a cot, bedding and a pram for the child'. This helpful description is taken from the opinion of Sheriff I. D. Macphail in *Freer* v *Taggart* 1975 SLT (Sh Ct) 13. The term would appear to be restricted to expenditure on the child. In the context of the 1930 Act inlying expenses would not extend to expenditure on the mother herself unless they were closely related to the needs of the child, there being no alimentary obligation owed by the father to the mother of an illegitimate child. In the context of s. 3 (1) (*b*) of the 1985 Act, it is suggested that a similar construction will be adopted. Any expenditure of a special nature incurred by the mother of a legitimate child for her own needs at or about the time of the birth would be recoverable under the general wording of the paragraph.

There are no financial limits on the amounts which may be recovered under either s. 3 (1) (*a*) or (*b*).

3. Power to backdate awards

For the first time the court is given power to award aliment for a period which has already elapsed (s. 3 (1) (*c*)). The court has power in all cases to award aliment from the date of raising the action. This is unlikely to become the normal practice, although the power could be useful where a wife had to incur debts or support herself at a subsistence level after she was deserted by her husband and before she was able to discover his whereabouts.

The court is also given power, on special cause shown, to award aliment for any earlier period. That special cause might be a wife's inability to trace a husband who had deliberately concealed his whereabouts. The power to backdate is without prejudice to any claim a person may have to be reimbursed for the past aliment of another person, on principles of unjustified enrichment (see p. 13).

Backdating is not effective for income tax purposes. In the English case of *Morley-Clarke* v *Jones* 1986 SLT 98; [1985] BTC 460, a 1980 order was backdated to 1969, in effect to substitute the child of the marriage for the spouse in order to enable a claim for repayment of tax to be made. The Court of Appeal held that the variation did not alter the fact that sums had been paid to the spouse under an obligation subsisting at the time of payment, and that the payments remained her income. Similarly, in *I.R. Commrs* v *Craw* [1985] 1 All ER 31; BTC 477, the First Division of the Court of Session held that a sheriff court order for aliment, which was stated to be backdated to the date of a voluntary separation agreement, had no bearing on what had actually happened as a matter of fact during the period prior to the making of the order. The payments during that period were made in consequence of the agreement alone, and, as a result of the Income and Corporation Taxes Act 1970, s. 437, were treated as the husband's income.

4. Other powers

The court has certain powers where either aliment or financial provision is being claimed; for example to make orders relating to avoidance transactions (p. 59): to grant warrant for inhibition or warrant for arrestment on the dependence of the action (p. 60); and to order a party to provide details of his resources (p. 61). The court is given no power to order security to be provided for the payment of aliment.

Quantification of Aliment

1. General principles

The Act sets out the general principles relating to the quantification of claims for aliment. Some of these – such as the needs and resources of the parties – simply restate well-known principles of the common law. The Act does, however, make certain important changes, notably where an alimentary debtor is supporting someone he is under no legal obligation to support.

An obligation of aliment is defined as an obligation to provide such support as is reasonable in the circumstances (s. 1 (2)). In assessing aliment, the court is to have regard to all the circumstances of the case, and in particular to the needs and resources of the parties and to their earning capacities (s. 4 (1) (*a*) and (*b*)).

Earning capacity is referred to separately, because 'resources' might be too narrow a phrase to encompass it – even though 'resources' is defined to mean present and foreseeable resources (s. 27 (1)). 'Needs' is similarly defined to mean present and foreseeable needs. Earning capacity is clearly an important factor, but the Act does not attempt to define it. It will include, where appropriate, matters such as the age, health, previous experience and employment prospects of each party. In particular, the Act does not offer guidance on when a party (whether debtor or creditor) ought to seek employment. In principle, the form of the proceedings should not affect the answer to this question, nor should the answer necessarily depend on the sex of the defender (although in many cases a mother who has the care of small children will have no earning capacity or a much reduced capacity). In other words, the same result should in principle be reached regardless of whether the proceedings are civil proceedings for aliment, proceedings against a liable relative for the recovery of expenditure on supplementary benefit (Supplementary Benefits Act 1976, s. 18), or a criminal prosecution under s. 25 of that Act for failure to aliment. There are signs, however, that in the last case the courts regard the offence as involving a species of strict liability, at any rate where the accused is a man rather than a woman (*Galt* v *Turner* 1981 SLT (Notes) 99).

2. Defender supporting persons to whom no obligation owed

The aspect of quantification on which the Act makes most change is where the defender is supporting one or more persons to whom he owes no obligation of aliment. The court is given a discretion to take account of these circumstances, where previously it had to disregard them (s. 4 (3) (a)). This provision is especially important in the new law because of the reduction in the categories of alimentary obligant. Under the previous law a person's responsibility to care for an aged parent was taken into account because there was a lifelong reciprocal obligation of support between them. Even though this obligation is now abolished, the court will be able to reach the same conclusion. If a man's estranged wife and children are being supported by the State, and he is supporting another woman and her children, his wife will not obtain aliment from him if, in practice, he has no superfluity of resources (see *Henry* v *Henry* 1972 SLT (Notes) 26). Whether s. 4 (3) (a) will have any relevance in a prosecution under the Supplementary Benefits Act 1976, s. 25 remains to be seen.

The Act refers to 'any support, financial or otherwise'. Thus a man, in the example just given, might be looking after a woman's children while she went out to work. This might be a perfectly reasonable arrangement, e.g. if her earning capacity was greater than his. In situations of this kind, of course, the express reference to earning capacity in s. 4 (1) is also relevant.

A second wife (or cohabitant) is under no alimentary obligation to a man's first wife. The Act does not create any such obligation. However, if a second wife is working the resources available to the family as a whole will be increased, and the man will have more spare resources of his own at his disposal for meeting his alimentary obligations. No order could be made directly against the second wife, and if she gave up work to defeat a claim made against her husband, there would be no sanction against her. This, needless to say, would not often be in her own financial interests.

There is no reason in principle why aliment for an illegitimate child should be paid at a lower rate than for a legitimate child. In principle this was the position under the previous law.

Conduct

Under the Act the court is not to take account of any conduct of a party unless it would be 'manifestly inequitable to leave it out of account' (s. 4 (3) (b)). The use of the word 'manifestly' seeks to make clear that conduct should only be taken into account, so as to reduce or deny an award, in exceptional circumstances. The object is to simplify the proceedings and to preclude an unpleasant investigation into the whole history of the parties' relationship. Moreover, the negative wording of the paragraph should preclude the inference that it is the normal professional duty of a legal adviser to lead evidence of misconduct. A further object is to achieve some degree of uniformity in approach between different courts. A court would still, of course, be able to resort to this provision in order, for example, to deny an award to a man who had constantly battered his wife (and vice versa). The provision should never operate penally so as to increase the liability of a defender on account of his misconduct – the assessment of his means and resources and of the pursuer's needs should depend upon more objective criteria.

Variation, Recall and Expiry of Decrees

Most statutory provisions (now repealed by the Act) which conferred jurisdiction to award aliment also conferred power to vary or recall an order. This was not done by the Conjugal Rights (Scotland) Amendment Act 1861, s. 9, so there was no express power to vary an award of aliment for a child in a divorce action. This oversight was in practice surmounted by the court reserving leave to apply for variation in the interlocutor awarding aliment. This will no longer be necessary.

1. Variation or recall

The Act confers a general power on the court to vary or recall an order on a material change of circumstances (s. 5 (1)). The phrase 'material change of circumstances' does not indicate a change in substance to the law (see e.g. *Jenkinson* v *Jenkinson* 1981 SLT 65, but see p. 44). The new power applies to decrees granted in an action brought before or after the commencement of the Act.

In Court of Session divorce procedure, applications for variation and recall are made by motion (Rule of Court 170 B (10)). In sheriff court ordinary cause (including divorce) procedure, such applications are made by minute (OCR 129). However, in sheriff court summary cause procedure, such applications must be made by summons (Act of Sederunt (Summary Cause Rules Sheriff Court) 1976, SI 476, r. 79). The court has power, pending determination of an application for variation or recall, to make interim orders (s. 5 (3)).

The same principles apply to an application for variation and recall as apply to the original decree (s. 5 (2)). Thus the court can backdate an order for variation or recall (see p. 23). This would benefit a husband whose wife had failed to disclose that she had taken up employment. The power will be exercisable in all cases from the date of the application, although this is unlikely to become the normal practice. The court would be able to order variation or recall, on special cause shown, from an earlier date. The same factors would be relevant in quantifying liability as are relevant when the original order is made. The court would therefore be able to award sums to meet alimentary needs of an occasional or special nature, and to award less than the amount claimed. The court is given specific power to order the repayment of any sums paid under a decree (s. 5 (4)).

There are 1984 rules of court simplifying the procedure for the variation or recall in the sheriff court of alimentary orders made in consistorial actions in the Court of Session. These rules replace those previously made under the Law Reform (Miscellaneous Provisions) (Scotland) Act 1966, s. 8 (SI 1970/720). Under the new system an application to the sheriff is commenced by initial writ and proceeds as an ordinary cause: see Act of Sederunt (Variation and Recall of Orders in Consistorial Causes) 1984 (1984 SLT (News) 151).

2. Expiry

A decree for aliment expires on the occurrence of any event specified in the decree (such as a child's sixteenth birthday) or of an event ending the legal obligation (such as divorce). In other circumstances (such as resumption of cohabitation) the decree will not automatically come to an end, but the material change of circumstances will justify an application for variation or recall. The parties will often not bother to seek the recall of a decree in these circumstances, although there will be no incentive to enforce it during any period when the parties have resumed cohabitation.

Summary Cause Procedure

Section 23 confirms the most recent updating of the Sheriff Courts (Civil Jurisdiction and Procedure) (Scotland) Act 1963, s. 3 (see SI 1985/626). It is competent to use the summary cause procedure where a claim by a wife or by a child over the age of eighteen does not exceed £70 per week and where the amount claimed on behalf of a child under the age of eighteen does not exceed £35 per week. The procedure cannot be used where there is additionally a substantive conclusion, such as separation or affiliation.

Subsections (2), (3) and (4) of s. 23 restate the present statutory provisions. Subsection (2) will, in any event, be repealed when the Civil Jurisdiction and Judgments Act 1982 is brought into effect.

Award of Aliment or Custody Where Divorce, etc. Refused

Section 21 contains a general power enabling the court to make an order for aliment, or an order regulating custody, education or access, where decree of divorce, nullity of marriage or separation is refused. Section 21 applies to nullity of marriage by virtue of s. 17 (1). The power is exercisable in the sheriff court in actions of divorce or separation.

Section 21 removes certain technical difficulties in the previous law. For example, it was held in *Gall* v *Gall* 1968 SC 332 that the Court of Session had no jurisdiction to deal with custody after the main action had been dismissed as irrelevant without proof. An order could thus only be made if the action was dismissed after proof on the merits had been allowed, or after decree of absolvitor had been granted. The court is also able to determine any dispute between the parties over their respective property rights (i.e. by making an incidental order under s. 14 (2) (*d*)).

Interim Aliment

'Interim aliment' now means only interim aliment *pendente lite* (i.e. pending disposal of the action: s. 6 (1)). The old technical meaning of interim aliment, as contrasted with 'permanent' aliment, is discarded. The Act retains the broad discretionary nature of the court's existing powers. Thus the court can award less than the sum sued for and may refuse to award interim aliment (s. 6 (2)) and may vary or recall an award. The same principles apply to the variation or recall of an award of interim aliment as apply to the original award (s. 6 (4)).

The range of powers available to the court in granting interim aliment is less extensive than the range of powers available at the stage of a final award (see s. 6. This is why the definition of 'aliment' in s. 27 (1) excludes aliment *pendente lite* or interim aliment under s. 6.) The court may award periodical payments payable only until the date of disposal of the action or such earlier date as the court may specify (s. 6 (3)). The court does not have interim power to award payment of lump sums to meet alimentary needs of an occasional or special nature or to backdate awards. The court may order either party to provide details of his resources (s. 20) – indeed it is at the stage of an application for interim aliment that this power is likely to prove to be most useful. A claim for interim aliment is competent in an action for aliment alone, or in actions for divorce, separation, declarator of marriage or declarator of nullity of marriage (s. 6 (1)). Either party to an action of declarator of nullity of marriage may claim interim aliment, even if that party denies the existence of the alimentary relationship (see Chapter 6). A party could also claim interim aliment in an action for divorce even if, on the face of the pleadings, there were no grounds for divorce. In such circumstances an award would often be regarded as inappropriate (see e.g. *Boyle* v *Boyle* 1977 SLT (Notes) 69).

4 Financial Provision on Divorce – the New Principles

Introduction

From 1964 the court had an unfettered discretion to award a capital sum, or a periodical allowance, or both on divorce (Succession (Scotland) Act 1964, s. 26), but only to the party innocent of a matrimonial offence. From 1977 an award could be made to either party (Divorce (Scotland) Act 1976, s. 5). Before the commencement of the 1985 Act no guidance was given to the courts as to the objective of financial provision. There was no clear-cut rule on the relevance of the applicant's conduct; on whether an award should recognize a wife's often unpaid contribution to the marriage; or on whether or when a husband should be liable to support his wife after divorce. There was, and is, no *obligation* of support between ex-spouses.

The Act recognizes that no single objective of financial provision will be sufficient to deal with every case. Instead, it sets out five principles, contained in s. 9 (1), on any one or more of which a claim may be based. These are not, however, fixed rules. They depend in differing degrees on the exercise of judicial discretion. Whatever figure the court arrives at, it is not obliged to make an unrealistic order. It is to have regard to the resources of the parties (s. 8 (2) (b)). It is not the purpose of the legislation to render husbands bankrupt.

The new principles apply only in actions for divorce raised after the commencement of the Act: see s. 27 (1) (definition of 'action'). A broadly similar approach is adopted towards the extended range of powers in divorce actions (see p. 41). There is, however, an element of retrospection in relation to agreements on financial provision (see Chapter 7).

The commentary in this Chapter generally assumes that the claimant will be the wife. This will, of course, be so in the vast majority of cases where a claim for financial provision is made, although the Act certainly does not preclude a claim by a husband. A husband might conceivably claim under s. 9 (1) (c) if he has custody of the children of the marriage.

Where the assessment of an award continues to fall within the proper exercise of a judge's discretion, it seems unlikely that the appellate courts will be readier to interfere than they are at present. The Inner House has consistently indicated its reluctance to interfere (see e.g. *Gray* v *Gray* 1968 SC 185, First Division; *McRae* v *McRae* 1979 SLT (Notes) 45, Second Division, an approach repeated robustly by the Second Division in *Hume* v *Hume*, 23 May 1985, unreported). Nevertheless, the scope for an appeal will no doubt be greater, simply because the scope of judicial discretion has been much reduced by the new legislation.

Sharing of Matrimonial Property

1. General

The first of the new principles is that the net value of the matrimonial property should be shared fairly between the parties to the marriage (s. 9 (1) (a)). The key idea is to share what is acquired by the parties' joint efforts or income during the effective period of the marriage. The court's power is not restricted to ordering the transfer of matrimonial property. It may order the satisfaction of an award out of any funds or assets belonging to the husband (s. 8 (1) (a)) even if they do not fall within the definition of matrimonial property in s. 10 (4).

2. Meaning of matrimonial property

Under s. 10 (4), 'matrimonial property' means all the property belonging to either or both of the parties at (usually) the date of final separation (see p. 34) which was acquired during the marriage. It also includes property acquired before the marriage in one special case – where it was acquired for use by the parties as a family home or as furniture or plenishings for such home. The reasons for including the home and furniture are that these items are more closely connected with the marriage than any other kind of property (and indeed are often purchased by an engaged couple before the marriage takes place) and, moreover, the house is generally the most valuable asset. While most married couples who buy a house take the title in joint names, there are some who do not, and it would lead to unfair results if even a small number of divorcing women were denied a share of the value of the home. On the other hand, a house acquired and occupied by one party before the mariage would not necessarily be regarded as matrimonial property simply because the parties happened to live in it after their marriage; everything will depend on the purpose for which the house was bought. Matrimonial property does not include property acquired at any time by way of gift or succession from a third party. Such property cannot be regarded as being acquired by the joint efforts of the parties.

One or both of the parties may have taken out life assurance, or have rights under occupational pension schemes or similar arrangements. Where such rights have been acquired wholly during the period from marriage to final separation, the value of these rights would constitute matrimonial property. In many cases these rights will have been built up partly before marriage, partly during the effective period of the marriage and partly after the date of final separation. In these cases only the proportion attributable to the period between the marriage and final separation is to be treated as matrimonial property (s. 10 (5)). The value of a life policy at the date of final separation will often be the surrender value, but a party would not be precluded from leading evidence that a higher value is appropriate (e.g. where a policy has only a short time to run, the discounted maturity value may be more realistic).

3. Net value of matrimonial property

It is the net value of the matrimonial property which is to be shared (s. 10 (2)). This means the value of the property at the date of final separation, after deduction of any debts. The debts to be deducted are any debts incurred by either party during the marriage, whether or not they are connected with an item of matrimonial property. Thus the debts would include not only a building society loan over the matrimonial home, but also a personal loan granted to a husband by his bank, and also outstanding tradesmen's accounts. If a debt has been incurred before the marriage, however, it is only to be deducted if it relates to an item of matrimonial property. An example would be a building society loan over a house bought before the marriage for use as a matrimonial home, or a hire-purchase debt over furniture bought before the marriage for use in the home. Any other kind of personal debt incurred by either party before the marriage would fall to be deducted from that party's share of the matrimonial property. This would cover, e.g., a loan over a flat bought by an apparently confirmed bachelor long before he contemplated marriage. These rules in effect follow the definition of matrimonial property.

After the date of final separation any actings by either party in relation to an item of matrimonial property should not benefit or prejudice the other party. If, for example, the wife is running a small business, any increase in its value after the date of final separation due to her own efforts should not benefit her husband. Conversely the neglect of an item of matrimonial property by one party should not prejudice the other party. In the latter case the court is never required to make an unrealistic or penal order: s. 8 (2) (*b*) provides that any order for financial provision should be reasonable having regard to the resources of the parties.

4. The norm of equal sharing

In general fair sharing means equal sharing (s. 10 (1)). For this purpose it is irrelevant to consider whether or not both parties were earning, or to take into account their respective incomes. If parties agree, as they often still do, that the husband should be the sole breadwinner for the family, and that the wife should manage the domestic household, her share of the matrimonial property should not be diminished. In particular, there is no room for the argument that a one-third share is the appropriate norm. There is no place for the previous practice of awarding perhaps a third of a husband's total assets to his wife. This practice probably arose after 1964 when the system of fixed legal rights applying in succession law was replaced by judicial discretion. Analogies with succession law are not helpful in the new scheme. The old common law division into thirds – a third to the wife etc. – applied only to moveable property. Succession law has to make provision for the rights of children, while the 1985 Act contains no rule that a child's property rights are affected on the divorce of his parents. Furthermore, there is no justification for awarding a wife less than half of the matrimonial property simply because she is also to receive a share of her husband's future income in the form of periodical payments – any claim she may have to a share of his future income will be based on quite separate grounds, such as the economic burden of looking after the children of the marriage.

5. Special circumstances justifying departure from equal sharing

The court is, however, given power to depart from the norm of equal sharing when this is 'justified by special circumstances' (s. 10 (1)). These words make clear that any such departure is to be the exception and not the rule. The Act gives five specific examples of special circumstances, but this list is not exhaustive (s. 10 (6)).

The parties' agreement

The parties may have agreed that a particular item of property should be treated as the separate property of one of them, or that the matrimonial property should be shared otherwise than in equal proportions. The terms in which title to property, such as the home, has been taken would not in themselves necessarily constitute an agreement – a house might have been bought at a time when it was more common to take the title in the husband's name alone. The court is able to take the agreement into account, without necessarily being bound by it. In context the reference to agreement should be regarded as meaning an agreement made before or during the marriage, rather than for the purposes of an imminent or current divorce action; this is because of the separate provision dealing with agreements on financial provision on divorce (s. 16). There seems little likelihood in practice of a conflict between the court's power under s. 10 (6), and its limited powers to police agreements on financial provision under s. 16. In particular, the power to cut down an agreement under s. 16 (1) (b) will be exercised, if at all, at the time when the court is considering the division of matrimonial property under s. 10 (see s. 16 (2) (b): p. 58).

Source of funds or assets

The object of the concept of matrimonial property is to share what is acquired by joint efforts or income. The Act does not state this in terms. Instead, it hauls into the definition of matrimonial property everything acquired otherwise than by way of gift or succession, and then gives the court a discretion to depart from the norm of equal sharing, on equitable grounds, where funds or assets were not derived from the income or efforts of the parties during the marriage. One obvious example where the court's discretion might be invoked would be where a party buys property during the marriage with funds owned before the marriage. The reason for striking a balance in this way is to avoid a rigid rule requiring tracing of property to its source in all disputed cases. Such a rule would often present formidable evidential problems and would create additional expense. There would often be arguments as to what extent property represented a replacement of an asset originally owned by one of the parties. There might have been several intermediate transactions, for example frequent changing of investments. This is not to say, of course, that arguments of this kind will not arise under the Act; they frequently will. However, s. 10 enables the court to take a broad axe to what would otherwise be an intractable problem. One important case where the court might wish to exercise its discretion would be where the source of the funds used to acquire property during the marriage was a gift from a third party such as a parent. (If the property itself rather than the funds used to purchase it was a gift, it would not be matrimonial property in terms of s. 10 (4).) It will, of course, be open to either party to adduce evidence of the source of any funds or assets whenever it is in the interests of that party to do so.

Destruction, etc. of property

A further specified factor is the destruction, dissipation or alienation of property by either party. This is also the most obvious example where conduct has adversely affected the financial resources which are relevant to the decision of the court on a claim for financial provision (see s. 11 (7) (a): p. 49). In these circumstances the court can take the conduct into account. There is no conflict between the specific factor in s. 10 (6) (c) and the general rule on conduct prescribed by s. 11 (7) (a).

Nature and use of property

The court can take into account the nature of the matrimonial property, the use made of it (including use for business purposes or as a matrimonial home) and the extent to which it is reasonable to expect it to be realised or divided or used as security. A husband's capital may be tied up in a business, farm, private company or pension scheme, and it may not be reasonable or practicable for it to be used as an immediate source of funds to enable a capital sum to be paid to his wife. Even if the asset could be sold, it might not fetch its full market value and the husband might be deprived of future income. The court is given power to depart from the norm of equal sharing, but it would be unnecessary to exercise this power if the problem could be resolved in some other way; for example by an order for a capital sum to be paid by instalments. In other words, the power is only likely to be exercised where it is impossible to reach a fair result by recourse to other provisions in the Act.

Similarly, the court would not necessarily have to award more than half the value of the matrimonial home to the wife simply because it was to remain the home of the children of the marriage. There is a danger that the supposed needs of the family could be used to justify results which would be unfair to the husband. There is no principle in the Act (as there used to be in England and Wales before the Matrimonial and Family Proceedings Act 1984) that the court is to attempt to place the parties in the financial position which they would have been in had the marriage not broken down (Matrimonial Causes Act 1973, s. 25 (1)). This is an unattainable object in the vast majority of cases. A number of alternative courses are open to the court. Where the house has sufficient value it will be possible for the parties to sell it and for each to purchase more modest accommodation. Where other property is available the court could order a counterbalancing payment in favour of the husband, in return for a transfer of his interest in the home to his wife. The court could make an order (under s. 14 (2) (*d*)), regulating the occupation of the matrimonial home and providing for a payment or transfer of property at some future date when the children cease to be dependent. (See e.g. *Hector* v *Hector* [1973] 1 WLR 1122.) In this connection factors such as inflation and interest would have to be taken into account. Where the court makes an order regulating occupancy alone, it retains the power to make an order for sale, or for determining any dispute over property rights, at a future date (see s. 14 (1), (2) (*a*) and (*c*)). Section 14 (1) specifically enables the court to make an incidental order after the granting of decree of divorce.

Liability for valuation and legal expenses

It is left to the court to adjust any share of matrimonial property in the light of the actual or prospective liability of either party for any expenses of valuation or transfer of property. This provision is limited to expenses relating to property disputes on divorce. The Act contains, in s. 22, a separate provision that the expenses of the divorce proceedings themselves are no longer to be regarded as necessaries for which the husband is liable (see p. 62).

6. Meaning of final separation

Normally there will be a single occasion when the parties separate, and it will be easy to ascertain the date. Sometimes, however, the parties may resume cohabitation in an attempt to rescue their marriage. A short resumption of cohabitation does not postpone the date of final separation. The Act lays down a somewhat arbitrary test in order to achieve a degree of certainty. Where the parties ceased to cohabit for 90 days or more, and thereafter resumed cohabitation for a period or periods of less than 90 days in all, the earlier date of separation is taken to be the date of final separation (s. 10 (7)). Otherwise no account is taken of any cessation of cohabitation followed by a resumption of cohabitation: the parties have not yet finally separated.

The concept of separation is expressed by the words 'ceased to cohabit'. Section 27 (2) provides that the parties to a marriage should be held to cohabit with one another only when they are in fact living together as man and wife. This is the same test as that contained in the Divorce (Scotland) Act 1976, s. 13 (2). It is theoretically possible for the parties to cease to cohabit even if they continue to live under the same roof though it will be difficult in practice to convince the court. Proof will be required, at the very least, that the parties did not have sexual relations; and probably also that a wife was no longer rendering certain domestic services which wives traditionally render to their husbands (see e.g. *Macdonald* v *Macdonald* 1948 SLT 380).

Where the parties are still cohabiting at the date of service of a summons in a divorce action, that date is taken as the date of final separation (s. 10 (3) (*b*)).

Economic Advantages and Disadvantages

The second principle laid down by the Act is that fair account should be taken of any economic advantage derived by either party from contributions by the other, and of any economic disadvantage suffered by either party in the interests of the other party or of the family (s. 9 (1) (*b*)).

The most obvious example of an economic disadvantage is where a well-qualified woman gives up her own career prospects in order to bring up her family. The longer the marriage lasts, the more difficult it will be for her to resume her career. At the very least she is likely to earn less than if she had not interrupted her career.

There are numerous examples of economic advantages derived from the other party's contribution. A husband may have paid off a loan over a house owned by his wife before marriage. A wife may have helped her husband build up his business, with little or no personal reward. A wife's unpaid domestic services may have enabled her husband to work long hours in order to further his career. These examples include both financial and non-financial contributions.

How would the application of this principle work in practice? It will almost certainly be the most difficult principle to quantify, but that by itself is no reason for ignoring the fact that, in certain circumstances, some compensation is due. The following points should be noted.

(1) The principle is only to be applied where a share of the value of the matrimonial property (and/or an award under some other principle) would not be sufficient

recognition of the economic advantages and disadvantages. In many cases a wife's contribution to the marriage will be adequately reflected in her share of the matrimonial property. If both parties have contributed to the welfare of the family, and if both have earning potential which is not affected by the marriage, sharing the matrimonial property will often produce a satisfactory result. This may not always be the case, especially if there is no matrimonial property or if it is of small value. The court is therefore directed to have regard to the extent to which any resulting imbalance has been or will be corrected by a sharing of the value of the matrimonial property or otherwise (s. 11 (2) (*b*)). The words 'or otherwise' include the application of the principles set out in s. 9 (1) (*c*), (*d*) and (*e*), or any agreement on financial provision between the parties.

(2) There may well be relevant contributions made and economic disadvantages sustained by both parties. The court is therefore directed to have regard to the extent to which the economic advantages or disadvantages sustained by either party have been balanced by the economic advantages or disadvantages sustained by the other party (s. 11 (2) (*a*)).

(3) The definition of 'contributions' in s. 9 (2) includes non-financial contributions. The principle is not, therefore, restricted to the case where a wife has contributed directly to the joint income of the parties during the marriage, for example by seeking employment herself or by assisting her husband in his business.

(4) In appropriate circumstances contributions made and economic disadvantages sustained before the marriage may be taken into account (s. 9 (2)). This makes suitable allowance for the kind of case where a long period of cohabitation is succeeded by a relatively short marriage. But the reference to marriage in the definitions of 'economic advantage' and 'contributions' (see s. 9 (2)) makes clear that there must at some stage be a marriage before a relevant claim for financial provision under this head may be made.

(5) This principle (in common with the sharing of matrimonial property) is looking to past, not future, contributions and disadvantages. It cannot be satisfied by an award of a periodical allowance (see s. 13 (2)). For this reason there is no reference to such factors as the needs and resources of the parties (which are relevant to claims under the remaining principles in s. 9 (1) (*c*), (*d*) and (*e*)). If, therefore, a wife's earning prospects have been seriously affected by the marriage, she will be entitled to claim a sum of money (payable, if necessary, by instalments), or a transfer of property or both, to compensate her for what happened during the period of the marriage. Additionally (or alternatively) the award might be satisfied by an incidental order, such as the right to occupy the home (s. 14 (2) (*d*)). In this case her husband might also be ordered to pay the outgoings on the house, such as the rates, loan repayments and maintenance costs (s. 14 (2) (*e*)). If a wife's earning capacity is so adversely affected (especially after a long marriage) that she cannot obtain suitable employment, she may well have an additional claim under principle (e) (see

p. 39), that is, for serious financial hardship suffered as a result of the divorce: a principle which concentrates on the future consequences of the divorce. There will in practice be an element of overlap between these two principles, even though they serve different purposes.

(6) Section 11 (7) (*a*) provides that the court shall not take account of the conduct of either party unless the conduct has adversely affected the financial resources which are relevant to the decision of the court on a claim for financial provision. Thus if a wife had failed to contribute in any way to the economic success of the marriage, the court could take this into account. Nevertheless, the court would no doubt be slow to encourage any argument that a wife was lazy in her performance of domestic chores. Such matters are particularly irrelevant in the case where a wife's future earning prospects have been affected by a joint decision that she should not work during the marriage. What the court could *not* do in any circumstances is to take account of a husband's allegation that his wife's misconduct – such as adultery, unreasonable behaviour or desertion – had caused the irretrievable breakdown of the marriage. Such misconduct is not of an economic character and is not therefore relevant to the assessment of an award under this principle. In short, the principle is not intended as a vehicle for rewarding 'good' conduct or for penalising 'bad' conduct.

Economic Burden of Child Care

The third principle is that any economic burden of caring, after divorce, for a child of the marriage under the age of sixteen years should be shared fairly between the parties (s. 9 (1) (*c*)). This principle is distinct from any claim for aliment by or on behalf of a child, but the court is directed to have regard to any decree for aliment or arrangement made by the parties themselves for the child's aliment (s. 11 (3) (*a*)). The principle recognizes that the burden of caring for young children will usually affect a wife's expenses or earning capacity. The Act does not attempt to specify when loss of earning capacity is the result of a need to care for a dependent child rather than of a voluntary decision not to work: this is left to depend on the circumstances of the case. There may be cases where a divorced mother could reasonably be expected to realise her full earning capacity when the children were, say, of primary school age; on the other hand there may be cases where some loss of earning capacity or extra expense such as child-care would continue even after the children were at secondary school. This principle does not necessarily have to be satisfied by the award of a periodical allowance; indeed, the court is directed by s. 13 (2) (*b*) not to make an order for a periodical allowance unless it is satisfied that an order for payment of a capital sum or for transfer of property would be inappropriate or insufficient. The principle might, for example, be satisfied by an incidental order (under s. 14 (2) (*d*)) regulating the occupation of the matrimonial home (s. 11 (3) (*c*) refers specifically to the need to provide suitable accommodation for the child).

Apart from the matters already referred to, the Act specifies a number of other factors to which the court should have regard. These are:

- the age and health of the child;
- the educational, financial and other circumstances of the child;
- the availability and cost of suitable child-care facilities or services;
- the needs and resources of the parties; and
- all the other circumstances of the case (s. 11 (3) (*d*)–(*h*)).

A 'child of the marriage' is defined by s. 27 (1) to include a child accepted by *both* parties as a child of the family. A husband would not be liable to his divorced wife under this principle if he himself had not accepted her child as a child of his family. The age of sixteen is selected in s. 9 (1) (*c*) *inter alia* because that is the age at which a decree awarding custody ceases to have effect.

The calculation of separate claims both for aliment for a child and financial provision for a divorced mother should not in practice be any more complex than the calculation of separate claims for aliment while the marriage still subsists. Often the husband will not have the resources adequately to meet both claims. In cases such as this the fact that aliment is being paid for the child will be significant (see the factor in s. 11 (3) (*a*)). If aliment for the child is paid on a generous scale, enabling a divorced mother to engage someone to look after her child and to find employment, her own claim for financial provision under this principle might often be disallowed. If a mother particularly wished to care for her child herself, her husband might seek to pay less for the child by way of aliment and more to his former wife by way of financial provision, without his total liability necessarily being increased.

A Three-Year Adjustment Period

The fourth principle is that a party who has been dependent to a substantial degree on the financial support of the other party should be awarded such financial provision as is reasonable to enable him or her to adjust, over a period of not more than three years from the date of the decree of divorce, to the loss of that support on divorce (s. 9 (1) (*d*)). Depending on the circumstances, the purpose of the award might be to enable a wife to undertake a course of training or retraining, or to give her time to find suitable employment, or to enable her to adjust gradually to a lower standard of living. The maximum period of three years is regarded as sufficient to provide for any necessary adjustment to independence after divorce. The period is to run from the date of decree of divorce, even where the award is made in terms of s. 12 (1) (*b*) or s. 13 (1) (*b*) or (*c*), after decree of divorce. An award under this principle need not take the form of a periodical allowance; indeed, the court is directed by s. 13 (2) (*b*) not to make an order for a periodical allowance unless it is satisfied that an order for payment of a capital sum or for transfer of property would be inappropriate or insufficient.

The factors to which the court is to have regard are:

- the age, health and earning capacity of the claimant;
- the duration and extent of the dependence of the claimant prior to divorce;
- any intention of the claimant to undertake a course of education or training;
- the needs and resources of the parties; and
- all the other circumstances of the case (s. 11 (4)).

A woman seeking financial provision under both this and the previous principle would not in practice obtain extra money from her husband during the first three years after divorce, except for such matters as tuition charges. Conduct is not to be taken into account unless it would be manifestly inequitable to leave it out of account (s. 11 (7) (*b*): see p. 49).

Serious Financial Hardship

The previous four principles would not always ensure that a wife who suffered serious financial hardship as a result of the divorce could recover some financial provision in appropriate cases. If there were no matrimonial property, no room for a claim based on contributions or disadvantages, and no dependent children, then a divorced wife (in the absence of any further head of claim) could be awarded at most a provision designed to ease her adjustment to independence over a period of not more than three years. A fifth principle is therefore needed. It is that a party who at the time of the divorce seems likely to suffer serious financial hardship as a result of the divorce should be awarded such financial provision as is reasonable to relieve him or her of hardship over a reasonable period (s. 9 (1) (*e*)).

The term 'serious financial hardship' indicates that an award under this principle should be the exception rather than the rule. It does not introduce a concept of continuing quasi-alimentary liability between spouses after divorce. An award under this principle will generally be appropriate only after a long marriage, where a divorcing wife is middle-aged or elderly, and her earning capacity much reduced. The principle excludes the possibility of an award on the ground of supervening hardship: only hardship which, at the time of divorce, seems likely to arise as a result of the divorce can be taken into account. It will not, therefore, be competent to apply to the court for an order if, perhaps years after divorce, an event unforeseen at the time of the divorce leads to a deterioration in a divorced wife's financial circumstances. This is designed to facilitate a 'clean break' between the parties. To some extent the rule is arbitrary. A wife paralysed as a result of a road accident six months before the divorce would have a claim for financial provision; a divorced wife who suffered a similar injury six months after the divorce would not. A wife whose progressive disease was diagnosed before the divorce would have a claim but a woman whose disease was first diagnosed after the divorce would not.

A later event which improves a wife's financial circumstances may, however, constitute a material change of circumstances, justifying an application by her former husband for variation or recall of an order for a periodical allowance (under s. 13 (4)).

An award need not take the form of a periodical allowance; indeed, the court is directed by s. 13 (2) (*b*) not to make an order for a periodical allowance unless it is satisfied that an order for payment of a capital sum or for transfer of property would be inappropriate or insufficient. A suitable form of award in many cases will be a capital sum payable by instalments (s. 12 (3)). If a periodical allowance is awarded, it need not be for an indefinite period (see s. 13 (3)). The wording of s. 13 (3) precludes the court from following the decision in *Chalmers* v *Chalmers* 1983 SLT 535.

The factors to which the court is to have regard are:

- the age, health and earning capacity of the claimant;
- the duration of the marriage;
- the standard of living of the parties during the marriage;
- the needs and resources of the parties; and
- all the other circumstances of the case (s. 11 (5)).

Conduct is not to be taken into account unless it would be manifestly inequitable to leave it out of account (s. 11 (7) (*b*): see p. 49).

5 Orders for Financial Provision on Divorce

Orders Which May be Made

Under the previous law the court's powers were very restricted. The court could make an order for the payment of a capital sum or a periodical allowance or both (Divorce (Scotland) Act 1976, s. 5). There was also a little-used power to set aside or vary the terms of a marriage settlement (s. 5 (1) (*c*)), and power to counteract avoidance transactions (1976 Act, s. 6). These last two powers are retained with modifications (ss. 14 (2) (*h*) and 18: see p. 47 and Chapter 8). Moreover the First Division of the Court of Session held that conditions could not be attached to an order for payment of a capital sum (e.g. that it should be payable by instalments instead of a single lump sum) or to an order for a payment of a periodical allowance, e.g. that it should be payable for a fixed period rather than until the death or remarriage of the pursuer (see *Chalmers* v *Chalmers* 1983 SLT 535). The 1985 Act greatly increases the scope of the court's powers. Either party to the marriage may apply to the court for one or more of the following orders:

(a) an order for the payment of a capital sum or the transfer of property;
(b) an order for a periodical allowance;
(c) an incidental order (s. 8 (1)).

The new powers are not available in an action raised before the commencement of the Act. (The relevant sections – 12, 13 and 14 – refer to orders under s. 8 (2). Section 8 (2) itself depends on s. 8 (1), which refers to an 'action for divorce'. 'Action', as defined in s. 27 (1), means an action brought after the commencement of the Act.) The Divorce (Scotland) Act 1976, s. 5 is expressly preserved in order to deal with actions brought before the commencement of the Act; and the court is given power, when making or varying an order under the 1976 Act, to make the order for a definite or indefinite period or until the happening of a specified event (s. 28 (3)); this is to counteract the effect of *Chalmers* (*supra*). The new provisions on variation of agreements, however, apply to agreements whenever made (see Chapter 7).

41

Orders for Payment of Capital Sum or Transfer of Property

The Act states that an order for a periodical allowance should not be made unless the court is satisfied that an order for payment of a capital sum or for transfer of property would be inappropriate or insufficient to give effect to the principles on financial provision laid down by the Act (s. 13 (2) (*b*)). It is thus the clear policy of the legislation that an order for financial provision should be fulfilled, wherever possible, by an order for payment of a capital sum or for the transfer of property. The expressions 'capital sum' and 'property' are not defined, except that property is defined in s. 27 (1) to exclude a tenancy transferable under the Matrimonial Homes (Family Protection) (Scotland) Act 1981, s. 13. The reason for this exclusion is that s. 13 of that Act already gives the court power to order the transfer of a tenancy of the matrimonial home on granting decree of divorce or nullity of marriage. An order can therefore be made for payment of a capital sum out of funds which had been disposed of by a husband in such a way that he still effectively controlled them. The court would not in practice make an order which was impossible to comply with, for example over property which the husband did not own or control.

The Act impliedly retains the principle of the previous law that an application for payment of a capital sum must be made before decree of divorce is granted (Divorce (Scotland) Act 1976, s. 5) and extends the principle to orders for the transfer of property (s. 12 (1)). The court is also given power to grant decree and continue the action for a specified time to allow financial provision to be dealt with (s. 12 (1) (*b*)): at present an order for payment of a capital sum can only be made when decree of divorce is granted.

The court is given two other important new powers. On making an order for payment of a capital sum or for transfer of property, it may stipulate that the order shall come into effect at a specified future date (s. 12 (2)). It may also order that a capital sum be paid by instalments (s. 12 (3)). These powers will be especially useful where assets may not be immediately available or realisable. The court will thus be able to achieve directly what it could previously achieve indirectly (and then only to a limited extent) by superseding extract for a brief period such as six months. This power was regularly used, e.g. to give a husband time to sell the matrimonial home and to pay his wife a capital sum from the proceeds. (There is no reason why the courts should not continue to use this power in the future.) Payment of a capital sum by instalments might be particularly appropriate if a husband is due to receive a lump sum under an occupational pension scheme at an ascertainable future date. This will no doubt become one of the most widely used powers under the new Act. These powers will also facilitate the stated policy of avoiding, wherever possible, awards in the form of a periodical allowance.

The court is not empowered to alter, in the future, the amount of liability already fixed. If, however, the circumstances of either party have materially changed, the court may accelerate or defer payment or transfer (s. 12 (4)), especially where the original order had provided for payments by instalments, and the payer had subsequently acquired funds which would enable him to discharge his liability, either immediately or in fewer instalments. It follows that the death or remarriage of either party does not affect the amount of liability, though the death of the husband will usually constitute a material change of circumstances which would enable the court to vary the date or method of payment or transfer.

Orders for Periodical Allowance

It is the clear policy of the legislation, expressed in s. 13, that an order for financial provision should be fulfilled, wherever possible, by an order for payment of a capital sum or for transfer of property (s. 13 (2)). The section seeks to reduce the scope for subsequent applications to the court where the circumstances of one of the parties change, or where inflation reduces the value of the original award of a periodical allowance.

The court cannot deal with the sharing of matrimonial property, or with economic advantages and disadvantages sustained during the marriage (i.e. principles (a) and (b) contained in s. 9(1) and described at pp. 30–37) by means of an order for a periodical allowance. In other cases an order for a periodical allowance is not to be made unless the court is satisfied that an order for payment of a capital sum or for transfer of property would be inappropriate or insufficient (s. 13 (2) (b)).

As under the previous law the court can make an order for a periodical allowance on granting decree of divorce. It is also given power to grant decree of divorce and continue the action for a specified time to allow financial provision to be dealt with (s. 13 (1) (a) and (b)). Section 13 restates, in a different form, powers which the court already had to entertain an application after decree of divorce. The court may make an order where there has been a change of circumstances (s. 13 (1) (c)) (for the meaning of this phrase, see the discussion below on s. 13 (4)). Section 13 (1) (c) does not deal with variation or recall of an existing order, which is dealt with by s. 13 (4).

An order for a periodical allowance must come to an end on the death or remarriage of the payee (s. 13 (7) (b), reaffirming the previous law). The court may stipulate that an order is for an indefinite period (in which case it terminates on the death or remarriage of the payee, unless previously recalled) or for a definite period (s. 13 (3)). Any order for a periodical allowance under s. 9 (1) (c) or (d) must, by the very nature of these principles, be for a definite period.

An order does not automatically cease on the death of the payer, but his death constitutes a material change of circumstances justifying a review of the order (s. 13 (7) (a)). By contrast, an order made in an English divorce action automatically ceases on the death of the payer (see Illustration 2 in Chapter 1).

Section 13 (4) provides that an application for variation or recall is competent on a 'material change of circumstances'. This preserves the principle of the previous law where, however, the phrase used was a 'change of circumstances' (Divorce (Scotland) Act 1976, s. 5 (4)). It is not clear what change in substance, if any, is achieved by the inclusion of the word 'material'. It will be noticed that the test in s. 13 (1) (c), already referred to, does not contain the word 'material'. The previous legislation used the same phrase in both contexts (1976 Act, s. 5 (3) and (4)). It may be further observed that on every other occasion where the Act uses this concept, the statutory phrase is a 'material change of circumstances' (ss. 5 (1), 7 (2), 13 (4)). There is a general presumption that, when Parliament uses two different forms of wording, two different results are intended. This being so, the courts may hold that the test in s. 13 (1) (c) remains the same – employing, as it does, the form of words in the 1976 Act – but that the test in s. 13 (4) is stiffer than it was. (If this happens, there are implications for the test for variation or recall of a decree of aliment: see s. 5 (1).) On the other hand, the courts may hold that the test in s. 13 (4) is the same as before: notwithstanding the language of the 1976 Act, the reported cases have tended to use the expression 'material' change of circumstances where an order has been varied or recalled (see e.g. *Jenkinson* v *Jenkinson* 1981 SLT 65). In this event the courts may well hold that it is now easier than before for an ex-wife to demonstrate a change in her own or her ex-husband's financial circumstances if she applies under s. 13 (1) (c).

It is difficult to comprehend why there should now be two different standards to determine substantially the same point. The puzzled reader will derive no assistance from the Scottish Law Commission's report, because the draft legislation appended thereto used the same phrase – a 'change of circumstances' – in both contexts.

What can be said with confidence is that in both contexts, the relevant circumstances will include cases where the order was or was not made on the basis of incorrect information or where, through inadvertence, the defender did not oppose the application (see e.g. *Galloway* v *Galloway* 1973 SLT (Notes) 84, Inner House).

The court has two new powers. The first (s. 13 (4) (c)) is to convert the order into an order for payment of a capital sum or for a transfer of property. This would be especially useful on the payer's death, especially as a periodical allowance is not automatically terminated on such an event. The second (s. 13 (4) (b), (6)) in consonance with the provisions relating to variation or recall of a decree for aliment (see ss. 3 and 5), empowers the court to backdate the variation or recall and to order repayment of sums paid.

The new legislation does not amount to an open-ended charter for husbands, who have already been divorced, to seek a judicial reassessment of their financial responsibilities. Where the action of divorce was raised before the commencement of the new legislation, any application for periodical allowance, or for variation or recall of an order for periodical allowance, will continue to be regulated by the previous law. There is one qualification – a court can make an order for a definite or an indefinite period or until the happening of a specified event (s. 28 (3)). Before an application can be made there must be a change of circumstances so that, at the very least, there has been a significant change in the actual earnings or potential earning capacity of one of the parties. In the absence of any such change it will not be open to an ex-husband to reapply to the court, simply because he wishes to have a fixed termination date placed on an existing order. Even where an application for review is competent, the court may be placed in some difficulty. The rationale of the previous order may have been that there was little or no capital at the husband's disposal and that the only practical way of adequately compensating his wife was by means of a long-term periodical allowance. The position now may be that the husband has some capital: but the court lacks the power to substitute a new order, requiring payment of a capital sum, for the old one. The only practical solution to problems of this kind is for the parties to reach agreement between themselves. There may often, of course, be circumstances where the court regards continuing payments as no longer justifiable, for example where the divorce took place many years before, and an ex-wife is now financially self-supporting.

Section 13 (5) provides, for the avoidance of doubt, that the same principles apply to an application for variation and recall etc. as apply to the original application for periodical allowance.

Incidental Orders

1. General

The court is given a very wide range of incidental powers to give effect to the principles in s. 9. These powers are contained in s. 14 (2). Any incidental order may be made before, on or after the granting or refusal of decree of divorce (s. 14 (1)) but the Court of Session may by Act of Sederunt make rules restricting the categories of incidental order which may be made *before* decree of divorce (s. 14 (7)). The power to make an incidental order after the granting of the original order for financial provision will be of greatest practical importance in relation to the occupancy of the matrimonial home (s. 14 (2) (*d*) and (*e*)). Variation or recall of an incidental order may be made on cause shown (s. 14 (4)) rather than on a material change of circumstances, because incidental orders may take various forms and may require to be varied in diverse circumstances. None of the incidental powers about to be described was previously available to the court, except those set out in s. 14 (2) (*g*) and (*h*) – viz. an order for payments to a trustee or curator bonis, and an order varying a marriage settlement.

2. Order for the sale of property

The court could previously bring pressure to bear on a party to sell property by making an order for payment of a capital sum. Now the court can achieve its aim directly (s. 14 (2) (*a*)). Normally, however, it will continue to make an order for a capital sum, because this will allow the payer to choose how to raise the necessary money. The new power would be useful, however, if the matrimonial home was to be used as a family home for the children of the marriage but was thereafter to be sold, with the proceeds being divided equally between the parties to the marriage.

3. Order for the valuation of property

In most cases it can be left to the parties to produce their own valuations. There may be cases, however, where it would be useful for the court to order an independent valuation, and s. 14 (2) (*b*) permits such an order to be made.

4. Order for resolving property disputes

The court may make an order determining any dispute between the parties to the marriage as to their respective property rights by means of a declarator or otherwise: e.g. by interdict or a decree ordaining the other party to produce accounts (s. 14 (2) (*c*)). It will thus be unnecessary to raise separate proceedings for this purpose.

5. Order regulating the occupation of the matrimonial home etc.

The court may make an order regulating the occupation of the matrimonial home, or the use of furniture and plenishings therein, or excluding either party from the home. Such an order can only be made on or after the granting of decree of divorce (s. 14 (3)). Until the divorce the position is regulated by the Matrimonial Homes (Family Protection) (Scotland) Act 1981. The use of the term 'matrimonial home', rather than 'family home' (which appears in s. 10 (4) (*a*)) is to enable certain provisions of the 1981 Act to be applied (by s. 14 (5)). The revised definition of 'matrimonial home' in s. 22 of the 1981 Act (introduced by the Law Reform (Miscellaneous Provisions) (Scotland) Act 1985) is incorporated into this Act by s. 27 (1).

This power, in s. 14 (2) (*d*), supplements the provisions of the 1981 Act, under which any similar order ceases to have effect on the termination of the marriage. A power of this kind is essential in certain cases in order to provide a home for the dependent children of the marriage (but see p. 34 about the dangers of excessive use of this power). An order relating to the furniture would generally be appropriate only as a short-term solution. In the long term it would usually be better to divide the ownership of the furniture between the parties.

The 1981 Act conferred certain subsidiary rights on a party who was granted the right to occupy the matrimonial home or to use furniture belonging to the other party. These subsidiary rights include effecting essential repairs and making essential payments such as rent, rates or repayment of loan instalments (1981 Act, s. 2 (1) and (2)); and making payments due under hire-purchase agreements etc. (s. 2 (5) (*a*)). The position where one party is granted a right to occupy the matrimonial home after divorce under this Act is essentially the same as that where a spouse has occupancy rights during marriage, and s. 14 (5) therefore applies the same solutions to the various practical problems which may arise. The court, by making an ancillary order under s. 14 (2) (*k*) can ensure that the rights of occupation in the matrimonial home and rights to use furniture and plenishings conferred by the court on a divorced spouse are protected against adverse dealings.

6. Order regulating the liability for outgoings thereon

The court may make an order regulating liability, as between the parties, for outgoings in respect of the matrimonial home or furniture or plenishings therein (s. 14 (2) (e)). Such an order can only be made on or after the granting of decree of divorce (s. 14 (3)); until divorce the position is regulated by the Matrimonial Homes (Family Protection) (Scotland) Act 1981. If the wife is given the right to occupy the matrimonial home it may also be appropriate to specify who should be responsible for the upkeep. She already has certain subsidiary rights even in the absence of a court order under the 1981 Act, s. 2. These include the right to pay rent, rates, secured loan instalments, essential repairs, and 'non-essential' repairs authorized by the court. There is no power to prejudice the rights of third parties.

7. Order for provision of security

The court may make an order that security should be given for any financial provision (s. 14 (2) (f)). This is phrased in very general terms. In practice, if such an order is to be made, the payer will usually be required to grant a standard security over a house or to convey property to trustees.

8. Order for payments to trustee or curator bonis

The court may make an order that payments should be made or property transferred to any curator bonis or trustee or other person for the benefit of a party to the marriage (s. 14 (2) (g)). This will be of use where the applicant is mentally ill (cf. Divorce (Scotland) Act 1976, s. 5 (1), which enabled payments to be made to the applicant 'or for his benefit'). Rules of court already provide for the appointment of a curator ad litem to represent the defender's interest in such a case (Rule of Court 167; OCR, r. 133).

9. Order varying a marriage settlement

The court may make an order setting aside or varying any term in an antenuptial or postnuptial marriage settlement (s. 14 (2) (h)). This provision restates in slightly different terms the previous power (Divorce (Scotland) Act 1976, s. 5 (1) (c)), which was rarely used. The new power is not restricted to a term taking effect on or after the termination of the marriage (1976 Act, s. 5 (1) (e), a phrase discussed by Lord

Sutherland in *Brodie* v *Brodie*, 30 May 1986, unreported.) The words 'an antenuptial or postnuptial marriage settlement' are used in order to distinguish such a settlement from an agreement on financial provision, where the court's power to vary is more restricted (see p. 57). The Act contains no definition of 'marriage settlement', except for the inclusion of a settlement by way of a policy of assurance under the Married Women's Policies of Assurance (Scotland) Act 1880, s. 2 (s. 14 (6)). The power to vary cannot be used to deprive children of their rights under marriage contracts, because the rights of third parties are protected by s. 15.

10. Order for payment of interest

The court may make an order as to the date from which any interest on any amount awarded should run (s. 14 (2) (*j*)). This should be useful in cases where one spouse has enjoyed, or will enjoy, the sole use of property in which the other has an interest; or where the court has awarded a capital sum payable at a future date or in instalments (s. 12 (2) and (3)). It may be appropriate to award interest from the date of citation, or decree, or from a future date, or even from a date prior to citation, e.g. where the matrimonial property was valued at the date of final separation. This could not be done at common law, under which the general rule governing illiquid claims is that interest can only be awarded from the date of the final decree (see e.g. *Macrae* v *Reed and Mallik Ltd* 1961 SC 68).

11. Ancillary orders

The court may make any other order which is expedient to give effect to the principles governing an award of financial provision or to any order for financial provision (s. 14 (2) (*k*)). This gives the court wide powers to make other incidental orders. These might include, for example, orders remitting a matter to a conveyancer, or directing a clerk of court to execute a deed, or authorizing a messenger-at-arms to take possession of, and deliver, corporeal moveables, or attaching conditions to any other order for financial provision.

Rights of Third Parties

Section 15 lays down two important rules. First, the court is precluded from making an order for the transfer of property if the necessary consent of a third party is not obtained (s. 15 (1)). For example, the transfer of shares in a private company is often dependent on the consent of the directors. Secondly, where the property is subject to security, the creditor must be given an opportunity to be heard by the court before it makes an order transferring the property (s. 15 (2)). The second rule does not provide an exception to the first. In all cases where the consent of a third party must, for whatever reason, be obtained, the court has no power to make an order unless that consent is given. Where, however, the consent of a secured creditor is not required he is still to be given an opportunity to be heard. The second rule is not confined to heritable property, although its main application in practice will be in that area. Neither an incidental order, nor any right conferred by such an order, is to prejudice any rights of any third party in so far as those rights existed immediately before the making of the order (s. 15 (3)). Thus an order giving a wife the right to occupy a home belonging to her former husband does not affect the rights of a building society or other heritable creditor having a right in security over the house.

Quantification of Financial Provision

Section 11 (6) contains a provision in similar terms to s. 4 (3) (*a*) (see p. 25). The court may, if it thinks fit, take account of the responsibilities of the party who is to make the financial provision towards any dependent member of his household, whether or not that member is a person to whom he owes an obligation of aliment. This provision is limited to claims for financial provision where an order for a periodical allowance is competent (i.e. the principles contained in s. 9 (1)(*c*), (*d*) and (*e*) described at pp. 37–40).

Form of Conclusion for Financial Provision

Practical problems may arise where a wife concludes for financial provision to be paid in a certain way and her husband offers to satisfy the claim in a different way. The wife may ask for a transfer of property or payment of a capital sum, and her husband may say that it is inconvenient to transfer that particular property or that he cannot raise the capital sum. An order for the payment of a capital sum by instalments will often be appropriate. In the Court of Session it is now possible to include a conclusion for 'such other order as the court may consider appropriate' (r. 156 (2) (*l*)). This will enable the court to adopt a flexible approach, and should preclude the need to amend the conclusion in the circumstances described above. There is no equivalent provision in the revised Ordinary Cause Rules applying to the sheriff court, but no doubt the court will be able to achieve the desired flexibility.

Relevance of Conduct

The approach of the Act is to examine the role of conduct separately in relation to each governing principle. In general a distinction is drawn between those principles which seek to recognize what has been 'earned' during the marriage, i.e. a share of the value of the matrimonial property, or a claim based on economic advantages and disadvantages; and those which are based on the relief of short or long term difficulty or hardship. In the former case conduct is to be relevant only if it has affected the economic basis of the claim (s. 11 (7) (*a*)). Thus an extreme form of misconduct which would justify reduction of a party's share in the value of the matrimonial property (under s. 9 (1) (*a*)) would be destruction, dissipation or alienation of property (see s. 10 (6) (*c*)). The role of conduct is implicit in the principle that fair account should be taken of economic advantages and disadvantages (s. 9 (1) (*b*)). In relation to the principle of sharing the economic burden of child-care (s. 9 (1) (*c*)), the responsibility of either party for the breakdown of the marriage is irrelevant: the justification for an award under this head is the assumption of the future care of a child of the marriage. In regard to the remaining principles, the test is the same as that for aliment laid down in s. 4 (3) (*b*): the court is not to take account of the conduct of either party unless it would be manifestly inequitable to leave it out of account (s. 11 (7) (*b*)). Where, say, a wife is solely responsible for the breakdown of the marriage, she cannot reasonably expect her husband to pay for any retraining or to continue to maintain her, perhaps indefinitely.

6 Nullity

General

Under the previous law, the court granting a decree of declarator of nullity had no discretionary power, as it did on granting decree of divorce, to order financial provision to be made to either party. As the theoretical effect of such a declarator is that the marriage has never existed, the court did have the limited power of restoring the parties so far as possible to their previous position, both in void and in voidable marriages (see *Mackle* v *Mackle* 1984 SLT 276).

The Act makes substantial alterations to the position at common law. The most important change is to give the court the same powers to award financial provision in nullity actions as in divorce actions (s. 17 (1)). 'Marriage' for this purpose means purported marriage (s. 27 (1)). No distinction is drawn between void and voidable marriages. Thus a woman may receive her share of the 'matrimonial' property, even though the 'marriage' was void from the outset. The reason is that, in both cases, the parties may have lived together as man and wife for years; either or both of them may have been unaware of any legal impediment to their marriage. The Act does not extend the jurisdiction of the sheriff court in nullity actions: the Court of Session retains exclusive jurisdiction. The provisions on nullity, as on divorce, apply only to actions brought after the commencement of the Act (s. 27 (1), definition of 'action').

'Marriage' in Scots law means the union of one man with one woman. The suggestion (*Scottish Law Gazette*, December 1985, p. 93) that s. 17 applies to failed homosexual relationships should therefore be disregarded.

Abolition of Common Law Rules

The Act also abolishes the mutual obligations to make restitution of property which were imposed by the common law (s. 17 (3)). At first sight these obligations might not appear inconsistent with the general scheme of the Act – the court could simply have taken into account the existence of these obligations, and indeed could have ordered the restitution of any property from one party to the other as part of the overall financial settlement. However, there were two potential areas of conflict between the common law and the Act which led to the abolition of the common law obligations. The first relates to conduct. In *Mackle* v *Mackle* 1984 SLT 276 it was suggested that the common law obligation arose only where property was transferred on the *faith* of the marriage, and that a person who knew of a bar to the marriage could not recover the property. Lord Kincraig did not have to decide this point, but thought (at p. 276) it had considerable force. It is submitted, however, that the suggestion has no substance. It seems clear that the institutional writers, in describing the position at common law, intended to do no more than describe the connecting link, the occasion when the transfer of property took place, i.e. the purported marriage. They refer to the obligation of restitution in unqualified terms (see Stair I. iv. 20; Erskine I. vi. 43). The form of wording used in decrees issued by the Consistorial Court – *propter nuptias* – and the later form of decree used in the Court of Session – *intuitu matrimonii . . . et propter nuptias* – justifies the same conclusion: see Fraser, *Husband and Wife* (2nd ed), p. 150. Whatever the true position at common law, it is clearly appropriate that the new statutory rules of conduct (s. 11 (7)) should apply without any qualification in nullity actions, especially as s. 11 (7) (*a*) would almost always preclude conduct from being taken into account in determining a share in the 'matrimonial' property.

The second potential area of conflict was also discussed in *Mackle* (at p. 277): the practical problems of determining, after many years, what must be restored and to whom. In view of the new statutory rules, the common law mutual obligations of restitution might have given rise to unnecessary complications and at best would have served no further useful purpose.

Interim Aliment

At common law it was not clear whether a person seeking, or not opposing, a declarator of nullity was entitled to seek interim aliment *pendente lite*. On a strict application of the principles of personal bar it is difficult to argue that a person who denies the existence of an alimentary relationship should be allowed to claim interim aliment. The Act removes this uncertainty by providing unequivocally that either party can seek interim aliment, irrespective of whether the marriage is void or voidable, and irrespective of the pleadings of either party (s. 6 (1)). It may perhaps seem artificial and contrary to principle to permit a party who denies the existence of the marriage to claim interim aliment, but the Act seeks to achieve simplicity of expression at the expense of undiluted principle. The justification for permitting either party to a nullity action to seek interim redress is that, whatever the outcome of the case, either party will be entitled to seek some form of financial provision from the other. If decree is granted, the court has power to award financial provision in the same way as on divorce; if decree is refused, the marriage continues and either party can claim aliment. There is, therefore, no reason to deprive either party of the right to seek interim redress, merely because that party denies the existence of the marriage. The Act does not offer the court specific guidance on whether a 'wife' should be awarded interim aliment in a nullity action where she and her husband have mutually agreed to live apart – this is a matter for interpretation of s. 2 (9) (see pp. 19–21).

Foreign Annulments

The recently enacted powers to make awards of financial provision after a foreign divorce, in certain exceptional circumstances (Matrimonial and Family Proceedings Act 1984, Pt. IV), are extended to foreign annulments, of whatever nature, of a purported marriage (1984 Act, s. 29 A, inserted by Sch. 1, para. 12 of the 1985 Act). Part IV of the 1984 Act also comes into force on 1 September 1986.

7 Agreements on Aliment and Financial Provision

Introduction

The Act contains two separate provisions on agreements – s. 7 deals with agreements on aliment, and s. 16 with agreements on financial provision. These provisions are not dissimilar. There are, however, a number of minor differences, due mainly to the fact that, in the case of aliment, the legal obligation of support continues. It is necessary to discuss separately alimentary agreements between husband and wife and alimentary agreements between parent and child.

Aliment – Husband and Wife

An agreement on aliment may be contained in a separation agreement, or may take the form of a contract or unilateral voluntary obligation designed for that specific purpose. Such an agreement is valid, if not challenged by either party. Either party may, however, revoke the agreement in certain circumstances. For example, a debtor husband may make an offer, which it is reasonable to expect his wife to accept, to take her back into his household and fulfil his obligation of aliment there (see the defence contained in s. 2 (8) and (9), which is expressly applied to agreements by s. 7 (3)). The Act does not make any change in substance to the revocability of agreements.

Before the Act came into force a provision in an agreement excluding recourse to the courts was thought to be of no effect, as being contrary to public policy (*Beaton* v *Beaton's Trs* 1935 SC 187, 195). The underlying philosophy of the Act is to encourage the parties to resolve questions of aliment between themselves. It does, however, recognize the need to protect persons who are in an economically weak position. Section 7 (1) therefore provides that any provision in an agreement which purports to exclude future liability for aliment, or to restrict any right to bring an action for aliment, shall have no effect unless the provision was fair and reasonable in all the circumstances of the agreement at the time it was entered into. There are no legislative guidelines on the question of reasonableness. The agreement may have sought to offer an adequate substitute for future alimentary liability, e.g. by transferring a capital sum or an item of property, such as the husband's interest in the matrimonial home. Agreements of this kind are more likely to satisfy the reasonableness test than those which undercompensate an alimentary creditor. The question of reasonableness has to be judged solely by reference to the facts which were known, or could reasonably have been anticipated, at the time of the agreement. To allow evidence to be led of subsequent events would be to create uncertainty and to detract from the advantages of seeking agreement. The wording, by implication, places the onus on the alimentary debtor to establish reasonableness – the provision has no effect until reasonableness is established.

There was uncertainty in the previous law as to whether the courts had power to vary amounts payable under an alimentary agreement. Thus a potential problem arose where a husband had not protected himself against the possibility of his own future indigence or of his wife's enhanced earning capacity. These problems are removed by s. 7 (2). Where an alimentary debtor enters into an agreement to pay aliment to or for the benefit of the creditor, either party may apply to the court on a material change of circumstances for variation of the amount payable or for the termination of the agreement. Thus payments which are strictly contractual will be subject to variation or recall, even if they exceed what a court might reasonably award by way of aliment, provided that they bear to be made for an alimentary purpose. What is or is not a material change in circumstances is not further explained – the rules of the common law continue to apply (but see the discussion at pp. 43–4). The alteration made by the Act to the nature of the alimentary relationship between spouses may also be of relevance in this context – the obligation is now fully reciprocal (see ss. 1 (1) (*a*) and (*b*), 4 (2); p. 7).

Aliment – Parent and Child

Before the Act came into force attempts by a parent to obtain a discharge of his future liability, or to exclude recourse to the courts, were of no effect. The position has been changed by the Act. Section 7 (1) applies to agreements between parent and child: any provision in an agreement which purports to exclude future liability for aliment or to restrict any right to bring an action for aliment shall have no effect unless the provision was fair and reasonable in all the circumstances of the agreement at the time it was entered into. Here, too, the agreement may have sought to offer an adequate substitute for future alimentary liability by, for example, transferring a capital sum. A father whose son was embarking on university education might prefer to give him a lump sum to cover the remaining years during which there might have been a continuing liability for aliment (i.e. until the son is twenty five at the latest – s. 1 (5) (*b*)). Here, too, agreements of this kind are more likely to satisfy the reasonableness test than those which make inadequate compensation. The observations at p. 56 apply to the facts to be taken into account in determining reasonableness, and to the question of onus of proof.

Section 7 (2) also applies to agreements between parent and child: on a material change of circumstances either party may apply to the court for variation of the amount payable or for termination of the agreement. This protects both a child who is obtaining too little and a parent who is paying too much. Under the previous law, where the alimentary obligation between parent and legitimate child was reciprocal, a parent might in theory have brought an action for aliment against his child in order to reduce his liability. This is no longer possible, as no child is now liable to aliment either of his parents.

What is or is not a material change of circumstances is not further explained – the common law rules continue to apply (but see the discussion at pp. 43–4).

Aliment – General

The new provisions relating to agreements on aliment are retrospective – they apply to an agreement entered into before or after the commencement of the Act. The expression 'agreement' includes a unilateral voluntary obligation (such as a bond of annuity by a husband in favour of his estranged wife: s. 7 (5)).

The court, in context, means the court which would have jurisdiction and competence to entertain an action for aliment between the parties to the agreement (s. 7 (4)). Without this provision there would have been uncertainty as to the grounds of jurisdiction in an action brought under s. 7 (2): such an action might not have been regarded as an action for aliment for the purposes of the Sheriff Courts (Scotland) Act 1907, s. 5 (2) (as amended by Sch.1, para. 1 of the 1985 Act).

A provision in an agreement, even if valid, does not affect the statutory liability of a person to maintain his spouse and children under the age of sixteen (Supplementary Benefits Act 1976, s. 17).

Financial Provision on Divorce

At common law a husband and wife had complete freedom to enter into an agreement on financial provision. A party could renounce rights to financial provision on divorce (see e.g. *Thomson* v *Thomson* 1982 SLT 521, First Division). There was no duty to refer an agreement to the court. There was no requirement that the court should approve its terms. The last three of these principles are retained: so is the first, subject to minor modification.

The underlying principle is that it is desirable to encourage parties to reach agreement between themselves and that the court should not become involved unless the parties cannot agree. As with agreements on aliment, however, the Act recognizes the need to protect the economically weaker party, who is generally the wife. Accordingly, s. 16 (1) (*b*) provides that, where the parties have entered into an agreement on financial provision, the court may make an order setting aside or varying the agreement or any term in it where the agreement was not fair and reasonable at the time it was entered into. There are no legislative guidelines as to factors which would be particularly important in determining the reasonableness of an agreement. Apart from the unequal bargaining strength of the parties, other obvious factors would be that a party was induced to enter into the agreement by threat or other unfair means; whether material facts were withheld; and whether both parties were legally represented. The Act would not preclude a party from challenging an agreement on some other ground, such as error, fraud, or force and fear.

Because of the need to achieve finality in the parties' financial affairs at the time of divorce (or very soon thereafter), the court's power to make such an order can only be exercised on granting decree of divorce or within such time thereafter as the court may specify on granting decree of divorce (s. 16 (2) (*b*)). The question of reasonableness has to be judged solely by reference to the facts which were known, or could reasonably have been anticipated, at the time of the agreement. To allow evidence to be led of subsequent events would be to create uncertainty and to detract from the advantages of seeking agreement. The wording by implication appears to place the onus of proof on the challenger to establish that the term is not fair and reasonable – the term is valid until set aside or varied by the court. On the question of onus of proof, therefore, the Act appears to lay down different rules for agreements on aliment and agreements on financial provision. Any attempt to exclude the right to apply to the court for an order is void (s. 16 (4)).

The Act confers on the courts another limited power to set aside or vary an agreement. This power may be exercised only where the agreement expressly so provides, and only where the term relates to a periodical allowance (s. 16 (1) (*a*)). (It is unlikely, in practice, that an agreement would ever provide expressly for variation of a term relating to payment of a capital sum or transfer of property.) The power may be exercised at any time after divorce (s. 16 (2) (*a*)). Any term in an agreement providing for the payment of a capital sum or the transfer of property must be challenged at the time of divorce.

The court also has power, on or at any time after granting decree of divorce, to set aside or vary any term of an agreement relating to periodical allowance in the event of the husband's insolvency (s. 16 (3)).

The new provisions are retrospective – they apply to an agreement entered into before or after the commencement of the Act (s. 16 (5)), provided always that the action is one to which the Act applies (i.e. the action has been raised on or after 1 September 1986). The Act does not regulate the situation where a decree is granted in terms of a joint minute. The effect, it is suggested, is that the joint minute is merged in, or superseded by, the decree and no longer has contractual effect.

8 Provisions Common to Both Aliment and Financial Provision

Orders Relating to Avoidance Transactions

Section 18 restates, with certain modifications, s. 6 of the Divorce (Scotland) Act 1976. The court continues to have power to counteract transactions intended to defeat claims for aliment and financial provision. The section is retrospective: it applies to claims made, in the appropriate range of actions, before the commencement of the Act (s. 18 (1)).

The new provisions are as follows. The court may exercise its powers in all actions for aliment or involving a claim for financial provision (or an application for variation or recall: s. 18 (1)). The range of actions is therefore broadened in two aspects. First, it extends to all actions for aliment, not merely actions for aliment between husband and wife, although the most important area of application will continue to be financial claims between spouses; and secondly, it extends to nullity actions as well as to divorce actions.

The court may make an order setting aside or varying any transfer of, or transaction involving, property effected by the other party not more than five years before the date of the making of the claim, or interdicting the other party from effecting any such transfer or transaction (s. 18 (1)). Thus transactions effected within a period of five years before the claim, instead of three years as under the previous law, are open to challenge. This change is made to protect spouses who may be divorced against their will on the basis of five years' non-cohabitation (Divorce (Scotland) Act 1976, s. 1 (2) (e)).

The section speaks of 'setting aside' rather than 'reducing' a transaction, because it has been suggested that the phrase 'reducing or varying' in the previous legislation confined it to written dispositions and transactions, so that it did not extend to, say, a gift of money (see *Maclean* v *Maclean* 1976 SLT 86). Similarly, the wording used to denote the type of transaction to which the clause refers has been broadened from 'any settlement or disposition of property' (1976 Act, s. 6) to 'any transfer of, or transaction involving, property'. The specific reference to interdicting the other party from transferring property furth of Scotland has been dropped as unnecessary (1976

59

Act, s. 6, as amended by Divorce Jurisdiction, Court Fees and Legal Aid (Scotland) Act 1983, Sch. 1, para. 21). The court may, if it is satisfied that the transfer or transaction had the effect of, or is likely to have the effect of, defeating in whole or part any claim, make the order applied for or such other order as it thinks fit (s. 18 (2)). The reference in the previous legislation to the intention of the transferor – 'wholly or partly for the purpose of defeating in whole or in part any claim' – has been removed and replaced by a purely objective test, viz. that the transfer or transaction 'had the effect of, or is likely to have the effect of, defeating in whole or in part' the claim.

The rights of a good faith third party acquirer for value are preserved by s. 18 (3), and are extended to cases where he has not yet acquired a real right; for example, where missives for the sale of heritable property have been concluded but a valid disposition has not yet been delivered.

The person seeking to have a transaction set aside must make averments sufficient to challenge the rights of a third party: either by alleging lack of good faith by the third party, or by alleging that the property was not acquired for value. Value does not necessarily mean full market value: it may vary according to the circumstances of the case. A donee is not protected by s. 18 (3) however innocent he may have been (see generally *Leslie* v *Leslie* 1983 SLT 186, per Lord Dunpark). In theory, each element contained in s. 18 (2) and (3) has to be considered separately, and different onera of proof attach to different elements. In practice, however, the provisions of the two subsections are likely to be considered together, and the most important factor is likely to be the proximity of relationship between the parties to the transaction. It will be rather difficult for a third party such as the husband's mother or current girlfriend to satisfy the court of good faith if, on the evidence, the value given is significantly less than the full market value. In theory, the third party has to establish *either* good faith (which is presumed in his favour, on general principles of law), *or* value; in practice these two elements will often be inextricably linked.

While a heritable creditor may be among the class of protected third parties, it seems unlikely that such a person would be able successfully to establish prejudice if an order were made: the dispute effectively relates only to the reversionary interest in the subjects (*Leslie* v *Leslie*, 26 July 1985, unreported, per Lord McCluskey).

The court is given power to include such terms and conditions as it thinks fit and to make any ancillary order which it considers expedient to ensure that the order is effective (s. 18 (4)).

Practical difficulties will occur where part or all of the relevant property is not situated in Scotland. It is beyond the scope of this book to explore the potential ramifications. Nonetheless the reader's attention is drawn to the Civil Jurisdiction and Judgments Act 1982 (which is expected to come into force shortly). Section 18 provides for the enforcement of UK judgments in other parts of the UK, and 'judgment' includes any judgment or order (by whatever name called) given or made by a court of law in the UK (s. 18 (2) (a)). The language appears to be wide enough to enable an interdict to be enforced in another part of the UK.

Inhibition and Arrestment

Under the previous law, the pursuer could not inhibit or arrest on the dependence of the action unless he averred special circumstances, such as that the defender was verging on insolvency, or was about to decamp (although inhibition is not restricted to these two cases: see *Wilson* v *Wilson* 1981 SLT 101). The court now has power, on cause shown, to grant warrant for inhibition or warrant for arrestment on the dependence of the action in which the claim is made and, if it thinks fit, to limit the inhibition to any particular property, or to limit the arrestment to any particular property or to funds not exceeding a specified value (s. 19 (1)). The power is available in all actions for aliment or involving a claim for financial provision, the most important area of application being financial claims between spouses. The power does not apply to applications for variation and recall, where it would be unnecessary. By adopting the test of showing cause it is intended that inhibition and arrestment should be easier to obtain than hitherto, thus reducing the need for interdict, which is a remedy of last resort and will still be available as such (see s. 18 (1) (ii)). A further alteration in the present law is to enable inhibition and arrestment to be restricted to specific items of property (such as the matrimonial home), or to a limited sum of money specified in the warrant.

Only the Court of Session has jurisdiction in relation to a warrant for inhibition; both the Court of Session and the sheriff court have jurisdiction in relation to a warrant for arrestment on the dependence (s. 19 (2)).

There is a general saving for the Law Reform (Miscellaneous Provisions) (Scotland) Act 1966, which ensures that wages, pensions etc. are to be exempt from arrestment on the dependence of an action (s. 19 (3)).

Provision of Details of Resources

In any action for aliment, or in any action which includes a claim for interim aliment or financial provision, the court may order either party to provide details of his resources or of those relating to a child or incapax on whose behalf he is acting (s. 20). It is envisaged that the court would not make an order *ex proprio motu*, but only on the application of a party to the action. Remedies were available under the previous law. A wife could claim an exorbitant amount to force her husband to furnish information. Alternatively she could seek a commission and diligence for the recovery of documents. This, however, can be expensive and has been discouraged by the courts where it is not clearly justified (see *Gould* v *Gould* 1966 SC 88; *Savage* v *Savage* 1981 SLT (Notes) 17). The court might simply decline to make an award until further information is provided. The section therefore permits the court to do directly what could only be done previously in a cumbersome or indirect way.

The court is not given power to make an order against anyone who is not a party to the action – such as a wealthy parent – and in this respect s. 20 reflects the existing approach of the courts (e.g. *Cassilis* v *Cassilis*, 29 October 1984, unreported). In extreme cases the failure of a party to provide details of his resources may constitute a criminal offence; and the courts can (and do) report such cases to the Crown Office for investigation (e.g. *Donnelly* v *Donnelly*, 1986 SLT 305 per Lord Ross, at p. 306).

Expenses of Action

Under the previous law, expenses incurred by a wife in conducting or contesting an action for divorce or other consistorial action were regarded as 'necessaries' for which her husband might be liable by virtue of his alimentary obligation towards her. Section 22 abolishes this rule and replaces it, in effect, with the wide discretion which the court already enjoys in awarding expenses in other actions. Section 22 accordingly provides that the expenses incurred by a party to a marriage in pursuing or defending certain actions should not be regarded as necessaries for which the other party to the marriage is liable. The actions referred to are:

(a) an action for aliment brought by either party to the marriage on his own behalf against the other party;

(b) an action for divorce, separation, declarator of marriage or declarator of nullity of marriage; or

(c) an application made after the commencement of the Act for variation or recall of a decree of aliment or an order for financial provision in an action brought before or after the commencement of the Act.

9 Matrimonial Property

Introduction

The Act contains three sections on certain aspects of the law of matrimonial property. They make only minor changes to the law. It should be noted that the term 'matrimonial property' appears only in the headnote to ss. 24–26, and does not mean the same as 'matrimonial property' for the purposes of financial provision on divorce.

Property Rights and Legal Capacity

Section 24 restates the principle of the law as it has stood since the Married Women's Property (Scotland) Acts 1881 and 1920: that the parties have separate property and independent legal capacity. The repeal of the relevant provisions in the 1881 and 1920 Acts does not, of course, have the effect of reviving the older law (Interpretation Act 1978, s. 16 (1)). 'Property' is not defined. It includes property of all kinds, including money and securities. The section does not affect any special statutory rules, such as occupancy rights in the matrimonial home. Nor does it affect the rule of law prohibiting, and rendering invalid, a marriage between parties one of whom is already married: this is to be regarded as an independent legal rule rather than a question of legal capacity. It does not affect the law of succession (s. 24 (2)).

Equal Shares in Household Goods

Section 25 introduces a presumption that a married couple's household goods are owned by them in equal shares. The presumption applies only to household goods obtained in prospect of or during the marriage other than by gift or succession from a third party; in other words, it does not in general apply to goods owned by either of the parties before marriage, on the analogy of the concept of 'matrimonial property' introduced for the purposes of financial provision on divorce (see p. 30).

'Household goods' means any goods (including decorative or ornamental goods) kept or used at any time during the marriage in any matrimonial home for the joint domestic purposes of the parties to the marriage, other than money or securities, any motor car, caravan or other road vehicle, or any domestic animal (s. 25 (3)). The definition of 'matrimonial home' in s. 27 (1) is the same as that now contained in the Matrimonial Homes (Family Protection) (Scotland) Act 1981, s. 22, by virtue of the Law Reform (Miscellaneous Provisions) (Scotland) Act 1985, s. 13 (10), and is used elsewhere in the new Act. The presumption would therefore normally apply only to goods in the matrimonial home while the parties are still living together.

The presumption is not rebutted merely because the goods were purchased by one or other of the parties or by both in unequal shares (s. 25 (2)). This is to prevent the presumption being affected by the mere accident that one party rather than the other happened to buy the goods. Otherwise the presumption will be rebutted by proof of actual ownership. It will also be rebutted by proof of purchase before marriage or during a period of separation.

Equal Shares in Money etc. from Housekeeping Allowance

Section 26 provides that money derived from any allowance made by either party for their joint household expenses or for similar purposes, or any property acquired out of such money, is to be treated in the absence of any agreement between them to the contrary as belonging to both parties in equal shares. The section thus extends the principle of the Married Women's Property Act 1964, s. 1 (which applied only to an allowance made by a husband to his wife) to allowances by either spouse.

Appendix I

Family Law (Scotland) Act 1985

ARRANGEMENT OF SECTIONS

Family Law (Scotland) Act 1985

Family Law (Scotland) Act 1985

(1985 Chapter 37)

An Act to make fresh provision in the law of Scotland regarding aliment; regarding financial and other consequences of decrees of divorce and of declarator of nullity of marriage; regarding property rights and legal capacity of married persons; and for connected purposes.

[*16th July 1985*]

Be it enacted by the Queen's most Excellent Majesty, by and with the advice and consent of the Lords Spiritual and Temporal, and Commons, in this present Parliament assembled, and by the authority of the same, as follows:

ALIMENT

S. 1   Obligation of aliment

1 (1)   [By whom obligation owed]   From the commencement of this Act, an obligation of aliment shall be owed by, and only by—

(*a*)   a husband to his wife;

(*b*)   a wife to her husband;

(*c*)   a father or mother to his or her child;

(*d*)   a person to a child (other than a child who has been boarded out with him by a local or other public authority or a voluntary organisation) who has been accepted by him as a child of his family.

1 (2)   [Meaning of obligation of aliment]   For the purposes of this Act, an obligation of aliment is an obligation to provide such support as is reasonable in the circumstances, having regard to the matters to which a court is required or entitled to have regard under section 4 of this Act in determining the amount of aliment to award in an action for aliment.

1 (3)   [Subsisting obligations]   Any obligation of aliment arising under a decree or by operation of law and subsisting immediately before the commencement of this Act shall, except insofar as consistent with this section, cease to have effect as from the commencement of this Act.

1 (4)   [Arrears]   Nothing in this section shall affect any arrears due under a decree at the date of termination or cessation of an obligation of aliment, nor any rule of law by which a person who is owed an obligation of aliment may claim aliment from the executor of a deceased person or from any person enriched by the succession to the estate of a deceased person.

1 (5)   [Interpretation]   In subsection (1) above—

'child' means a person—

(*a*)   under the age of 18 years; or

(*b*)   over that age and under the age of 25 years who is reasonably and appropriately undergoing instruction at an educational establishment, or training for employment or for a trade, profession or vocation;

'husband' and 'wife' include the parties to a valid polygamous marriage.

S. 2   Actions for aliment

2 (1)   [Jurisdiction]   A claim for aliment only (whether or not expenses are also sought) may be made, against any person owing an obligation of aliment, in the Court of Session or the sheriff court.

2 (2)   [Claim in other proceedings]   Unless the court considers it inappropriate in any particular case, a claim for aliment may also be made, against any person owing an obligation of aliment, in proceedings—

   (*a*)   for divorce, separation, declarator of marriage or declarator of nullity of marriage;

   (*b*)   relating to orders for financial provision;

   (*c*)   concerning rights and obligations in relation to children;

   (*d*)   concerning parentage or legitimacy;

   (*e*)   of any other kind, where the court considers it appropriate to include a claim for aliment.

2 (3)   [Interpretation]   In this Act **'action for aliment'** means a claim for aliment in proceedings referred to in subsection (1) or (2) above.

2 (4)   [By whom action may be brought]   An action for aliment may be brought—

   (*a*)   by a person (including a child) to whom the obligation of aliment is owed;

   (*b*)   by the curator bonis of an incapax or the curator of a minor who is an incapax;

   (*c*)   on behalf of a child under the age of 18 years, by—

      (i)   the father or mother of the child;

      (ii)   the tutor of a pupil;

      (iii)   a person entitled to, seeking or having custody or care of a child.

2 (5)   [Unborn child]   A woman (whether married or not) may bring an action for aliment on behalf of her unborn child as if the child had been born, but no such action shall be heard or disposed of prior to the birth of the child.

2 (6)   [Defender in same household]   It shall be competent to bring an action for aliment, notwithstanding that the person for or on behalf of whom aliment is being claimed is living in the same household as the defender

2 (7)   [Defence to action]   It shall be a defence to an action for aliment brought by virtue of subsection (6) above that the defender is fulfilling the obligation of aliment, and intends to continue doing so.

2 (8)   [Offer to receive into defender's household]   It shall be a defence to an action for aliment by or on behalf of a person other than a child under the age of 16 years that the defender is making an offer, which it is reasonable to expect the person concerned to accept, to receive that person into his household and to fulfil the obligation of aliment.

2 (9)   [Relevant factors]   For the purposes of subsection (8) above, in considering whether it is reasonable to expect a person to accept an offer, the court shall have regard among other things to any conduct, decree or other circumstances which appear to the court to be relevant: but the fact that a husband and wife have agreed to live apart shall not of itself be regarded as making it unreasonable to expect a person to accept such an offer.

2 (10)   [Receipt for aliment paid]   A person bringing an action for aliment under subsection (4) (*c*) above may give a good receipt for aliment paid under the decree in the action.

S. 3   Powers of court in action for aliment

3 (1)   [Powers of court]   The court may, if it thinks fit, grant decree in an action for aliment, and in granting such decree shall have power—

(*a*) to order the making of periodical payments, whether for a definite or an indefinite period or until the happening of a specified event;

(*b*) to order the making of alimentary payments of an occasional or special nature, including payments in respect of inlying, funeral or educational expenses;

(*c*) to backdate an award of aliment under this Act—

    (i) to the date of the bringing of the action or to such later date as the court thinks fit; or

    (ii) on special cause shown, to a date prior to the bringing of the action;

(*d*) to award less than the amount claimed even if the claim is undisputed.

3 (2) **[No power to substitute lump sum]** Nothing in subsection (1) above shall empower the court to substitute a lump sum for a periodical payment.

S. 4 Amount of aliment

4 (1) **[Relevant factors]** In determining the amount of aliment to award in an action for aliment, the court shall, subject to subsection (3) below, have regard—

(*a*) to the needs and resources of the parties;

(*b*) to the earning capacities of the parties;

(*c*) generally to all the circumstances of the case.

4 (2) **[Two or more parties owing obligation]** Where two or more parties owe an obligation of aliment to another person, there shall be no order of liability, but the court, in deciding how much, if any, aliment to award against any of those persons, shall have regard, among the other circumstances of the case, to the obligation of aliment owed by any other person.

4 (3) **[Circumstances of the case]** In having regard under subsection (1) (c) above generally to all the circumstances of the case, the court—

(*a*) may, if it thinks fit, take account of any support, financial or otherwise, given by the defender to any person whom he maintains as a dependant in his household, whether or not the defender owes an obligation of aliment to that person; and

(*b*) shall not take account of any conduct of a party unless it would be manifestly inequitable to leave it out of account.

S. 5 Variation or recall of decree of aliment

5 (1) **[Power to vary or recall]** A decree granted in an action for aliment brought before or after the commencement of this Act may, on an application by or on behalf of either party to the action, be varied or recalled by an order of the court if since the date of the decree there has been a material change of circumstances.

5 (2) **[Application of the Act]** The provisions of this Act shall apply to applications and orders under subsection (1) above as they apply to actions for aliment and decrees in such actions, subject to any necessary modifications.

5 (3) **[Interim order]** On an application under subsection (1) above, the court may, pending determination of the application, make such interim order as it thinks fit.

5 (4) **[Backdated order]** Where the court backdates an order under subsection (1) above, the court may order any sums paid under the decree to be repaid.

S. 6 Interim aliment

6 (1) **[Competence of claim]** A claim for interim aliment shall be competent—

(*a*) in an action for aliment, by the party who claims aliment against the other party;

(*b*) in an action for divorce, separation, declarator of marriage or declarator of nullity of marriage, by either party against the other party,

on behalf of the claimant and any person on whose behalf he is entitled to act under section 2(4) of this Act.

6 (2) **[Powers of court]**   Where a claim under subsection (1) above has been made, then, whether or not the claim is disputed, the court may award by way of interim aliment the sum claimed or any lesser sum or may refuse to make such an award.

6 (3) **[Expiry]**   An award under subsection (2) above shall consist of an award of periodical payments payable only until the date of the disposal of the action in which the award was made or such earlier date as the court may specify.

6 (4) **[Variation or recall of award]**   An award under subsection (2) above may be varied or recalled by an order of the court; and the provisions of this section shall apply to an award so varied and the claim therefor as they applied to the original award and the claim therefor.

S. 7   Agreements on aliment

7 (1) **[Unfair agreement to have no effect]**   Any provision in an agreement which purports to exclude future liability for aliment or to restrict any right to bring an action for aliment shall have no effect unless the provision was fair and reasonable in all the circumstances of the agreement at the time it was entered into.

7 (2) **[Change of circumstances]**   Where a person who owes an obligation of aliment to another person has entered into an agreement to pay aliment to or for the benefit of the other person, on a material change of circumstances application may be made to the court by or on behalf of either person for variation of the amount payable under the agreement or for termination of the agreement.

7 (3) **[Application of s. 2(8) and (9)]**   Subsections (8) and (9) of section 2 of this Act (which afford a defence to an action for aliment in certain circumstances) shall apply to an action to enforce such an agreement as is referred to in subsection (2) above as they apply to an action for aliment.

7 (4) **['The court']**   In subsection (2) above **'the court'** means the court which would have jurisdiction and competence to entertain an action for aliment between the parties to the agreement to which the application under that subsection relates.

7 (5) **['Agreement']**   In this section **'agreement'** means an agreement entered into before or after the commencement of this Act and includes a unilateral voluntary obligation.

FINANCIAL PROVISION ON DIVORCE, ETC.

S. 8   Orders for financial provision

8 (1) **[Orders which may be sought]**   In an action for divorce, either party to the marriage may apply to the court for one or more of the following orders—

(*a*) an order for the payment of a capital sum or the transfer of property to him by the other party to the marriage;

(*b*) an order for the making of a periodical allowance to him by the other party to the marriage;

(*c*) an incidental order within the meaning of section 14 (2) of this Act.

8 (2) **[Order to be made]**   Subject to sections 12 to 15 of this Act, where an application has been made under subsection (1) above, the court shall make such order, if any, as is—

(*a*) justified by the principles set out in section 9 of this Act; and

(*b*) reasonable having regard to the resources of the parties.

8 (3) [**'Order for financial provision'**]   An order under subsection (2) above is in this Act referred to as an 'order for financial provision'.

S. 9   Principles to be applied

9 (1) [**Principles**]   The principles which the court shall apply in deciding what order for financial provision, if any, to make are that—

   (*a*)   the net value of the matrimonial property should be shared fairly between the parties to the marriage;

   (*b*)   fair account should be taken of any economic advantage derived by either party from contributions by the other, and of any economic disadvantage suffered by either party in the interests of the other party or of the family;

   (*c*)   any economic burden of caring, after divorce, for a child of the marriage under the age of 16 years should be shared fairly between the parties;

   (*d*)   a party who has been dependent to a substantial degree on the financial support of the other party should be awarded such financial provision as is reasonable to enable him to adjust, over a period of not more than three years from the date of the decree of divorce, to the loss of that support on divorce;

   (*e*)   a party who at the time of the divorce seems likely to suffer serious financial hardship as a result of the divorce should be awarded such financial provision as is reasonable to relieve him of hardship over a reasonable period.

9 (2) [**Interpretation**]   In subsection (1) (*b*) above and section 11 (2) of this Act—

   '**economic advantage**' means advantage gained whether before or during the marriage and includes gains in capital, in income and in earning capacity, and '**economic disadvantage**' shall be construed accordingly;

   '**contributions**' means contributions made whether before or during the marriage; and includes indirect and non-financial contributions and, in particular, any such contribution made by looking after the family home or caring for the family.

S. 10   Sharing of value of matrimonial property

10 (1) [**Property to be shared fairly**]   In applying the principle set out in section 9 (1) (*a*) of this Act, the net value of the matrimonial property shall be taken to be shared fairly between the parties to the marriage when it is shared equally or in such other proportions as are justified by special circumstances.

10 (2) [**Net value**]   The net value of the matrimonial property shall be the value of the property at the relevant date after deduction of any debts incurred by the parties or either of them—

   (*a*)   before the marriage so far as they relate to the matrimonial property, and

   (*b*)   during the marriage,

which are outstanding at that date.

10 (3) [**'Relevant date'**]   In this section '**the relevant date**' means whichever is the earlier of—

   (*a*)   subject to subsection (7) below, the date on which the parties ceased to cohabit;

   (*b*)   the date of service of the summons in the action for divorce.

10 (4) [**'Matrimonial property'**]   Subject to subsection (5) below, in this section and in section 11 of this Act '**the matrimonial property**' means all the property belonging to the parties or either of them at the relevant date which was acquired by them or him (otherwise than by way of gift or succession from a third party)—

(*a*) before the marriage for use by them as a family home or as furniture or plenishings for such home; or

(*b*) during the marriage but before the relevant date.

10 (5)   [Life policy, pension etc.]   The proportion of any rights or interests of either party under a life policy or occupational pension scheme or similar arrangement referable to the period to which subsection (4) (*b*) above refers shall be taken to form part of the matrimonial property.

10 (6)   ['Special circumstances']   In subsection (1) above **'special circumstances'**, without prejudice to the generality of the words, may include—

(*a*) the terms of any agreement between the parties on the ownership or division of any of the matrimonial property;

(*b*) the source of the funds or assets used to acquire any of the matrimonial property where those funds or assets were not derived from the income or efforts of the parties during the marriage;

(*c*) any destruction, dissipation or alienation of property by either party;

(*d*) the nature of the matrimonial property, the use made of it (including use for business purposes or as a matrimonial home) and the extent to which it is reasonable to expect it to be realised or divided or used as security;

(*e*) the actual or prospective liability for any expenses of valuation or transfer of property in connection with the divorce.

10 (7)   [Resumption of cohabitation]   For the purposes of subsection (3) above no account shall be taken of any cessation of cohabitation where the parties thereafter resumed cohabitation, except where the parties ceased to cohabit for a continuous period of 90 days or more before resuming cohabitation for a period or periods of less than 90 days in all.

S. 11   Factors to be taken into account

11 (1)   [Application]   In applying the principles set out in section 9 of this Act, the following provisions of this section shall have effect.

11 (2)   [Economic factors]   For the purposes of section 9 (1) (*b*) of this Act, the court shall have regard to the extent to which—

(*a*) the economic advantages or disadvantages sustained by either party have been balanced by the economic advantages or disadvantages sustained by the other party, and

(*b*) any resulting imbalance has been or will be corrected by a sharing of the value of the matrimonial property or otherwise.

11 (3)   [Aliment or care for child]   For the purposes of section 9 (1) (*c*) of this Act, the court shall have regard to—

(*a*) any decree or arrangement for aliment for the child;

(*b*) any expenditure or loss of earning capacity caused by the need to care for the child;

(*c*) the need to provide suitable accommodation for the child;

(*d*) the age and health of the child;

(*e*) the educational, financial and other circumstances of the child;

(*f*) the availability and cost of suitable child-care facilities or services;

(*g*) the needs and resources of the parties; and

(*h*) all the other circumstances of the case.

11 (4)   [Circumstances of party claiming]   For the purposes of section 9 (1) (*d*) of this Act, the court shall have regard to—

(*a*) the age, health and earning capacity of the party who is claiming the financial provision;

(*b*) the duration and extent of the dependence of that party prior to divorce;

(*c*) any intention of that party to undertake a course of education or training;

(*d*) the needs and resources of the parties; and

(*e*) all the other circumstances of the case.

11 (5) **[Circumstances of party likely to suffer hardship]** For the purposes of section 9 (1) (*e*) of this Act, the court shall have regard to—

(*a*) the age, health and earning capacity of the party who is claiming the financial provision;

(*b*) the duration of the marriage;

(*c*) the standard of living of the parties during the marriage;

(*d*) the needs and resources of the parties; and

(*e*) all the other circumstances of the case.

11 (6) **[Support given to other dependant]** In having regard under subsections (3) to (5) above to all the other circumstances of the case, the court may, if it thinks fit, take account of any support, financial or otherwise, given by the party who is to make the financial provision to any person whom he maintains as a dependant in his household whether or not he owes an obligation of aliment to that person.

11 (7) **[Conduct]** In applying the principles set out in section 9 of this Act, the court shall not take account of the conduct of either party unless—

(*a*) the conduct has adversely affected the financial resources which are relevant to the decision of the court on a claim for financial provision; or

(*b*) in relation to section 9 (1) (*d*) or (*e*), it would be manifestly inequitable to leave the conduct out of account.

S. 12 Orders for payment of capital sum or transfer of property

12 (1) **[When order may be made]** An order under section 8 (2) of this Act for payment of a capital sum or transfer of property may be made—

(*a*) on granting decree of divorce; or

(*b*) within such period as the court on granting decree of divorce may specify.

12 (2) **[Prospective order]** The court, on making an order referred to in subsection (1) above, may stipulate that it shall come into effect at a specified future date.

12 (3) **[Instalments]** The court, on making an order under section 8 (2) of this Act for payment of a capital sum, may order that the capital sum shall be payable by instalments.

12 (4) **[Variation of the order]** Where an order referred to in subsection (1) above has been made, the court may, on an application by either party to the marriage on a material change of circumstances, vary the date or method of payment of the capital sum or the date of transfer of property.

S. 13 Orders for periodical allowance

13 (1) **[When order may be made]** An order under section 8 (2) of this Act for a periodical allowance may be made—

(*a*) on granting decree of divorce;

(*b*) within such period as the court on granting decree of divorce may specify; or

(*c*) after decree of divorce where—

(i) no such order has been made previously;

   (ii) application for the order has been made after the date of decree; and

   (iii) since the date of decree there has been a change of circumstances.

13 (2) **[Restrictions]** The court shall not make an order for a periodical allowance under section 8(2) of this Act unless—

   (*a*) the order is justified by a principle set out in paragraph (*c*), (*d*) or (*e*) of section 9 (1) of this Act; and

   (*b*) it is satisfied that an order for payment of a capital sum or for transfer of property under that section would be inappropriate or insufficient to satisfy the requirements of the said section 8 (2).

13 (3) **[Duration of order]** An order under section 8 (2) of this Act for a periodical allowance may be for a definite or an indefinite period or until the happening of a specified event.

13 (4) **[Change of circumstances]** Where an order for a periodical allowance has been made under section 8 (2) of this Act, and since the date of the order there has been a material change of circumstances, the court shall, on an application by or on behalf of either party to the marriage or his executor, have power by subsequent order—

   (*a*) to vary or recall the order for a periodical allowance;

   (*b*) to backdate such variation or recall to the date of the application therefor or, on cause shown, to an earlier date;

   (*c*) to convert the order into an order for payment of a capital sum or for a transfer of property.

13 (5) **[Application]** The provisions of this Act shall apply to applications and orders under subsection (4) above as they apply to applications for periodical allowance and orders on such applications.

13 (6) **[Backdated order]** Where the court backdates an order under subsection (4) (*b*) above, the court may order any sums paid by way of periodical allowance to be repaid.

13 (7) **[Death of party]** An order for a periodical allowance made under section 8 (2) of this Act—

   (*a*) shall, if subsisting at the death of the party making the payment, continue to operate against that party's estate, but without prejudice to the making of an order under subsection (4) above;

   (*b*) shall cease to have effect on the remarriage or death of the party receiving payment, except in relation to any arrears due under it.

S. 14   Incidental orders

14 (1) **[When order may be made]** Subject to subsection (3) below, an incidental order may be made under section 8 (2) of this Act before, on or after the granting or refusal of decree of divorce.

14 (2) **['Incidental order']** In this Act, **'an incidental order'** means one or more of the following orders—

   (*a*) an order for the sale of property;

   (*b*) an order for the valuation of property;

   (*c*) an order determining any dispute between the parties to the marriage as to their respective property rights by means of a declarator thereof or otherwise;

   (*d*) an order regulating the occupation of the matrimonial home or the use of furniture and plenishings therein or excluding either party to the marriage from such occupation;

   (*e*) an order regulating liability, as between the parties, for outgoings in respect of the matrimonial home or furniture or plenishings therein;

(*f*) an order that security shall be given for any financial provision;

(*g*) an order that payments shall be made or property transferred to any curator bonis or trustee or other person for the benefit of the party to the marriage by whom or on whose behalf application has been made under section 8 (1) of this Act for an incidental order;

(*h*) an order setting aside or varying any term in an antenuptial or postnuptial marriage settlement;

(*j*) an order as to the date from which any interest on any amount awarded shall run;

(*k*) any ancillary order which is expedient to give effect to the principles set out in section 9 of this Act or to any order made under section 8 (2) of this Act.

14 (3) **[Order only on or after divorce]** An incidental order referred to in subsection (2) (*d*) or (*e*) above may be made only on or after the granting of decree of divorce.

14 (4) **[Variation or recall]** An incidental order may be varied or recalled by subsequent order on cause shown.

14 (5) **[Matrimonial home]** So long as an incidental order granting a party to a marriage the right to occupy a matrimonial home or the right to use furniture and plenishings therein remains in force then—

(*a*) section 2 (1), (2), (5) (*a*) and (9) of the Matrimonial Homes (Family Protection) (Scotland) Act 1981 (which confer certain general powers of management on a spouse in relation to a matrimonial home), and

(*b*) subject to section 15 (3) of this Act, section 12 of the said Act of 1981 and section 41 of the Bankruptcy (Scotland) Act 1985 (which protect the occupancy rights of a spouse against arrangements intended to defeat them),

shall, except to the extent that the order otherwise provides, apply in relation to the order—

(i) as if that party were a non-entitled spouse and the other party were an entitled spouse within the meaning of section 1 (1) or 6 (2) of the said Act of 1981 as the case may require;

(ii) as if the right to occupy a matrimonial home under that order were 'occupancy rights' within the meaning of the said Act of 1981; and

(iii) with any other necessary modifications; and

subject to section 15 (3) of this Act, section 11 of the said Act of 1981 (protection of spouse in relation to furniture and plenishings) shall apply in relation to the order as if that party were a spouse within the meaning of the said section 11 and the order were an order under section 3 (3) or (4) of the said Act of 1981.

History
S. 14 (5) (b) amended by Bankruptcy (Scotland) Act 1985, Sch. 7, para. 23 by substituting reference to s. 41 of that Act for former reference to ss. 30 (as modified for the purposes of s. 31A), 31A and 76A of the Bankruptcy (Scotland) Act 1913, with effect from 1 April 1986.

14 (6) **['Settlement']** In subsection (2) (*h*) above, **'settlement'** includes a settlement by way of a policy of assurance to which section 2 of the Married Women's Policies of Assurance (Scotland) Act 1880 relates.

14 (7) **[Power to make rules]** Notwithstanding subsection (1) above, the Court of Session may by Act of Sederunt make rules restricting the categories of incidental order which may be made under section 8 (2) of this Act before the granting of decree of divorce.

S. 15 Rights of third parties

15 (1) **[Consent of third party]** The court shall not make an order under section 8 (2) of this Act for the transfer of property if the consent of a third party which is necessary under any obligation, enactment or rule of law has not been obtained.

15 (2) **[Consent of creditor]** The court shall not make an order under section 8 (2) of this Act for the transfer of property subject to security without the consent of the creditor unless he has been given an opportunity of being heard by the court.

15 (3) **[Rights not prejudiced]** Neither an incidental order, nor any rights conferred by such an order, shall prejudice any rights of any third party insofar as those rights existed immediately before the making of the order.

S. 16 Agreements on financial provision

16 (1) **[Power to set aside or vary]** Where the parties to a marriage have entered into an agreement as to financial provision to be made on divorce, the court may make an order setting aside or varying—

   (a) any term of the agreement relating to a periodical allowance where the agreement expressly provides for the subsequent setting aside or variation by the court of that term; or

   (b) the agreement or any term of it where the agreement was not fair and reasonable at the time it was entered into.

16 (2) **[When order may be made]** The court may make an order—

   (a) under subsection (1) (a) above at any time after granting decree of divorce; and

   (b) under subsection (1) (b) above on granting decree of divorce or within such time thereafter as the court may specify on granting decree of divorce.

16 (3) **[Bankruptcy etc.]** Without prejudice to subsections (1) and (2) above, where the parties to a marriage have entered into an agreement as to financial provision to be made on divorce and—

   (a) the estate of the party by whom any periodical allowance is payable under the agreement has, since the date when the agreement was entered into, been sequestrated, the award of sequestration has not been recalled and the party has not been discharged;

   (b) an analogous remedy within the meaning of section 10 (5) of the Bankruptcy (Scotland) Act 1985 has, since that date, come into force and remains in force in respect of that party's estate; or

   (c) that party's estate is being administered by a trustee acting under a voluntary trust deed granted since that date by the party for the benefit of his creditors generally or is subject to an analogous arrangement,

the court may, on or at any time after granting decree of divorce, make an order setting aside or varying any term of the agreement relating to the periodical allowance.

16 (4) **[Any exclusion void]** Any term of an agreement purporting to exclude the right to apply for an order under subsection (1) (b) or (3) above shall be void.

16 (5) **['Agreement']** In this section, **'agreement'** means an agreement entered into before or after the commencement of this Act.

S. 17 Financial provision on declarator of nullity of marriage

17 (1) **[Application]** Subject to the following provisions of this section, the provisions of this Act shall apply to actions for declarator of nullity of marriage as they apply to actions for divorce; and in this Act, unless the context otherwise requires, **'action for divorce'** includes an action for declarator of nullity of marriage and, in relation to such an action, **'decree'** and **'divorce'** shall be construed accordingly.

17 (2) **[Interim claim competent]** In an action for declarator of nullity of marriage, it shall be competent for either party to claim interim aliment under section 6 (1) of this Act notwithstanding that he denies the existence of the marriage.

17 (3) **[Restitution of property]** Any rule of law by virtue of which either party to an action for declarator of nullity of marriage may require restitution of property upon the granting of such declarator shall cease to have effect.

SUPPLEMENTAL

S. 18 Orders relating to avoidance transactions

18 (1) **[Rights of claimant]** Where a claim has been made (whether before or after the commencement of this Act), being—

(a) an action for aliment,

(b) a claim for an order for financial provision, or

(c) an application for variation or recall of a decree in such an action or of an order for financial provision,

the party making the claim may, not later than one year from the date of the disposal of the claim, apply to the court for an order—

(i) setting aside or varying any transfer of, or transaction involving, property effected by the other party not more than 5 years before the date of the making of the claim; or

(ii) interdicting the other party from effecting any such transfer or transaction.

18 (2) **[Power to make order]** Subject to subsection (3) below, on an application under subsection (1) above for an order the court may, if it is satisfied that the transfer or transaction had the effect of, or is likely to have the effect of, defeating in whole or in part any claim referred to in subsection (1) above, make the order applied for or such other order as it thinks fit.

18 (3) **[Rights of third party]** An order under subsection (2) above shall not prejudice any rights of a third party in or to the property where that third party—

(a) has in good faith acquired the property or any of it or any rights in relation to it for value; or

(b) derives title to such property or rights from any person who has done so.

18 (4) **[Conditions and ancillary orders]** Where the court makes an order under subsection (2) above, it may include in the order such terms and conditions as it thinks fit and may make any ancillary order which it considers expedient to ensure that the order is effective.

S. 19 Inhibition and arrestment

19 (1) **[Power to grant warrant]** Where a claim has been made, being—

(a) an action for aliment, or

(b) a claim for an order for financial provision,

the court shall have power, on cause shown, to grant warrant for inhibition or warrant for arrestment on the dependence of the action in which the claim is made and, if it thinks fit, to limit the inhibition to any particular property or to limit the arrestment to any particular property or to funds not exceeding a specified value.

19 (2) **['The court']** In subsection (1) above, **'the court'** means the Court of Session in relation to a warrant for inhibition and the Court of Session or the sheriff, as the case may require, in relation to a warrant for arrestment on the dependence.

19 (3) **[Exemption]** This section is without prejudice to section 1 of the Law Reform (Miscellaneous Provisions) (Scotland) Act 1966 (wages, pensions, etc. to be exempt from arrestment on the dependence of an action).

S. 20 Provision of details of resources

20 In an action—

(*a*) for aliment;

(*b*) which includes a claim for an order for financial provision; or

(*c*) which includes a claim for interim aliment,

the court may order either party to provide details of his resources or those relating to a child or incapax on whose behalf he is acting.

S. 21 Award of aliment or custody where divorce or separation refused

21 A court which refuses a decree of divorce or separation shall not, by virtue of such refusal, be prevented from making an order for aliment or an order regulating custody or education of, or access to, a child or an incidental order determining any dispute between the parties as to their respective property rights.

S. 22 Expenses of action

22 The expenses incurred by a party to a marriage in pursuing or defending—

(*a*) an action for aliment brought by either party to the marriage on his own behalf against the other party;

(*b*) an action for divorce, separation, declarator of marriage or declarator of nullity of marriage;

(*c*) an application made after the commencement of this Act for variation or recall of a decree of aliment or an order for financial provision in an action brought before or after the commencement of this Act,

shall not be regarded as necessaries for which the other party to the marriage is liable.

S. 23 Actions for aliment of small amounts

23 For section 3 of the Sheriff Courts (Civil Jurisdiction and Procedure) (Scotland) Act 1963 there shall be substituted the following section—

'Actions for aliment of small amounts

3(1) An action under section 2 of the Family Law (Scotland) Act 1985 for aliment only (whether or not expenses are also sought) may be brought before the sheriff as a summary cause if the aliment claimed in the action does not exceed—

(*a*) in respect of a child under the age of 18 years, the sum of £35 per week; and

(*b*) in any other case, the sum of £70 per week;

and any provision in any enactment limiting the jurisdiction of the sheriff in a summary cause by reference to any amount, or limiting the period for which a decree granted by him shall have effect, shall not apply in relation to such an action.

3(2) Without prejudice to any other enactment, the sheriff shall have jurisdiction in an action for aliment brought as a summary cause by virtue of subsection (1) above if—

(*a*) the pursuer resides within the jurisdiction of the sheriff, and

(*b*) the action could, by virtue of section 6 of the principal Act (which relates to jurisdiction), have been brought in the sheriff court of another sheriffdom.

3(3) The Lord Advocate may by order vary the amounts prescribed in paragraphs (*a*) and (*b*) of subsection (1) above.

3(4) The power to make an order under subsection (3) above shall be exercisable by statutory instrument subject to annulment in pursuance of a resolution of either House of Parliament and shall include power to vary or revoke any order made thereunder.'

MATRIMONIAL PROPERTY, ETC.

S. 24 Marriage not to affect property rights or legal capacity

24 (1) **[Effect of marriage]** Subject to the provisions of any enactment (including this Act), marriage shall not of itself affect—

(*a*) the respective rights of the parties to the marriage in relation to their property;

(*b*) the legal capacity of the parties to the marriage.

24 (2) **[Succession]** Nothing in subsection (1) above affects the law of succession.

S. 25 Presumption of equal shares in household goods

25 (1) **[Presumption]** If any question arises (whether during or after a marriage) as to the respective rights of ownership of the parties to a marriage in any household goods obtained in prospect of or during the marriage other than by gift or succession from third party, it shall be presumed, unless the contrary is proved, that each has a right to an equal share in the goods in question.

25 (2) **[Proof of contrary]** For the purposes of subsection (1) above, the contrary shall not be treated as proved by reason only that while the parties were married and living together the goods in question were purchased from a third party by either party alone or by both in unequal shares.

25 (3) **['Household goods']** In this section **'household goods'** means any goods (including decorative or ornamental goods) kept or used at any time during the marriage in any matrimonial home for the joint domestic purposes of the parties to the marriage, other than—

(*a*) money or securities;

(*b*) any motor car, caravan or other road vehicle;

(*c*) any domestic animal.

S. 26 Presumption of equal shares in money and property derived from housekeeping allowance

26 If any question arises (whether during or after a marriage) as to the right of a party to a marriage to money derived from any allowance made by either party for their joint household expenses or for similar purposes, or to any property acquired out of such money, the money or property shall, in the absence of any agreement between them to the contrary, be treated as belonging to each party in equal shares.

GENERAL

S. 27 Interpretation

27 (1) **[Interpretation]** In this Act, unless the context otherwise requires—

'action' means an action brought after the commencement of this Act;

'action for aliment' has the meaning assigned to it by section 2 (3) of this Act;

'aliment' does not include aliment *pendente lite* or interim aliment under section 6 of this Act;

'caravan' means a caravan which is mobile or affixed to the land;

'**child**' includes an illegitimate child, and any reference to the child of a marriage (whether or not subsisting) includes a child (other than a child who has been boarded out with the parties, or one of them, by a local or other public authority or a voluntary organisation) who has been accepted by the parties as a child of the family;

'**the court**' means the Court of Session or the sheriff, as the case may require;

'**decree**' in an action for aliment includes an order of the court awarding aliment;

'**family**' includes a one-parent family;

'**incidental order**' has the meaning assigned to it by section 14 (2) of this Act;

'**marriage**', in relation to an action for declarator of nullity of marriage, means purported marriage;

'**matrimonial home**' has the meaning assigned to it by section 22 of the Matrimonial Homes (Family Protection) (Scotland) Act 1981;

'**needs**' means present and foreseeable needs;

'**obligation of aliment**' shall be construed in accordance with section 1 (2) of this Act;

'**order for financial provision**' means an order under section 8 (2) of this Act and, in sections 18 (1) and 22 (*c*) of this Act, also includes an order under section 5 (2) of the Divorce (Scotland) Act 1976;

'**party to a marriage**' and '**party to the marriage**' include a party to a marriage which has been terminated or annulled;

'**property**' in sections 8, 12, 13 and 15 of this Act does not include a tenancy transferable under section 13 of the Matrimonial Homes (Family Protection) (Scotland) Act 1981;

'**resources**' means present and foreseeable resources;

'**voluntary organisation**' means a body, other than a local or other public authority, the activities of which are not carried on for profit.

27 (2) **[Cohabitation]** For the purposes of this Act, the parties to a marriage shall be held to cohabit with one another only when they are in fact living together as man and wife.

S. 28 Amendments, repeals and savings

28 (1) **[Amendments]** The enactments specified in Schedule 1 to this Act shall have effect subject to the amendments set out therein.

28 (2) **[Repeals]** The enactments specified in columns 1 and 2 of Schedule 2 to this Act are repealed to the extent specified in column 3 of that Schedule.

28 (3) **[Saving]** Nothing in subsection (2) above shall affect the operation of section 5 (orders for financial provision) of the Divorce (Scotland) Act 1976 in relation to an action for divorce brought before the commencement of this Act; but in the continued operation of that section the powers of the court—

(*a*) to make an order for payment of periodical allowance under subsection (2) thereof; and

(*b*) to vary such an order under subsection (4) thereof,

shall include power to make such an order for a definite or an indefinite period or until the happening of a specified event.

S. 29 Citation, commencement and extent

29 (1) **[Citation]** This Act may be cited as the Family Law (Scotland) Act 1985.

29 (2) **[Entry into operation]** This Act shall come into operation on such day as the Secretary of State may appoint by order made by statutory instrument, and different days may be appointed for different purposes.

29 (3) **[Transitional provisions]** An order under subsection (2) above may contain such transitional provisions and savings as appear to the Secretary of State necessary or expedient in connection with the provisions brought into force (whether wholly or partly) by the order.

29 (4) **[Extent]** So much of section 28 of, and Schedule 1 to, this Act as affects the operation of the Maintenance Orders Act 1950 and the Maintenance Orders (Reciprocal Enforcement) Act 1972 shall extend to England and Wales and to Northern Ireland as well as to Scotland, but save as aforesaid this Act shall extend to Scotland only.

Schedules

Schedule 1 — Minor and Consequential Amendments

Section 28 (1)

THE SHERIFF COURTS (SCOTLAND) ACT 1907 (c. 51)

1 In section 5 of the Sheriff Courts (Scotland) Act 1907 (jurisdiction), for subsection (2) there shall be substituted the following subsection—

'**(2)** Actions for aliment or separation (other than any action mentioned in subsection (2A) below) and actions for regulating the custody of children:'.

THE GUARDIANSHIP OF INFANTS ACT 1925 (c. 45)

2 In section 3 (3) of the Guardianship of Infants Act 1925 (orders for custody and access not enforceable while parents living together), for the words from the beginning to the word 'accrue' there shall be substituted the words 'No such order for custody or education shall be enforceable'.

THE MAINTENANCE ORDERS ACT 1950 (c. 37)

3 In section 16 (2) (*b*) (i) of the Maintenance Orders Act 1950 (enforcement of maintenance orders in other parts of the United Kingdom), at the end there shall be added the words 'or an order for financial provision in the form of a monetary payment under section 8 of the Family Law (Scotland) Act 1985'.

THE SUCCESSION (SCOTLAND) ACT 1964 (c. 41)

4 In section 33 (2) of the Succession (Scotland) Act 1964 (construction of references to legal rights in marriage contracts), at the end there shall be added the words 'or section 8 of the Family Law (Scotland) Act 1985'.

THE LAW REFORM (MISCELLANEOUS PROVISIONS) (SCOTLAND) ACT 1966 (c. 19)

5 In section 8 (1) of the Law Reform (Miscellaneous Provisions) (Scotland) Act 1966 (variation and recall of certain orders regarding custody and maintenance), at the end of paragraph (*c*) there shall be added the words 'or section 8 of the Family Law (Scotland) Act 1985'.

THE MAINTENANCE ORDERS (RECIPROCAL ENFORCEMENT) ACT 1972 (c. 18)

6 In section 31 of the Maintenance Orders (Reciprocal Enforcement) Act 1972 (application by person in convention country for recovery of maintenance in Scotland—

(*a*) for subsections (1A) there shall be substituted the following subsections—

'**(1A)** Proceedings arising out of an application under subsection (1) above shall be treated as an action for aliment within the meaning of the Family Law (Scotland) Act 1985 and, subject to subsections (1B) to (1D) below, the provisions of that Act relating to aliment shall apply in relation to claims for maintenance in such proceedings and decrees therein.

(1B) Without prejudice to subsection (2) below, any proceedings mentioned in sub-section (1A) above shall be brought in the sheriff court.

(1C) In its application to proceedings mentioned in subsection (1A) above, section 5 of the said Act of 1985 (power to vary or recall decree of aliment) shall be subject to section 34 (1) of this Act.

(1D) Where an application under subsection (1) above is for the recovery of main-tenance from a person who is a former spouse of the applicant—

(*a*) then, for the purposes of the said Act of 1985, there shall be assumed to be an obligation of aliment within the meaning of that Act owed by the former spouse to the applicant;

(*b*) section 2 (7) and (8) of that Act shall not apply; and

(*c*) an order for payment of maintenance in proceedings arising out of the application—

(i) shall, if subsisting at the death of the party making the payment, continue to operate against that party's estate, but without prejudice to the power of the court to vary or recall the order; and

(ii) shall cease to have effect on the remarriage or death of the party receiving payment, except in relation to any arrears due under it';

(*b*) after subsection (4) there shall be inserted the following new subsection—

'**(4A)** In subsection (4) (i) above the reference to the dissolution of a marriage by divorce shall be construed as including a reference to the annulment of a purported marriage and any reference to a marriage, a divorce, a divorced person, a former spouse or divorce proceedings shall be construed accordingly.'; and

(*c*) subsection (5) shall cease to have effect.

7   In section 39 of that Act, in the definition of 'maintenance', for the words 'as a periodical allowance' there shall be substituted the words 'by one former spouse for the support of the other'.

THE MATRIMONIAL PROCEEDINGS (POLYGAMOUS MARRIAGES) ACT 1972 (c. 38)

8   In section 2 (2) of the Matrimonial Proceedings (Polygamous Marriages) Act 1972 (decrees in respect of polygamous marriages)—

(*a*) for paragraphs (*d*) and (*e*) there shall be substituted the following paragraphs—

'(*d*) a decree of separation;

(*e*) a decree of aliment;'; and

(*b*) after the word 'ancillary' there shall be inserted the words 'or incidental'.

THE DOMICILE AND MATRIMONIAL PROCEEDINGS ACT 1973 (c. 45)

9   In Schedule 2 to the Domicile and Matrimonial Proceedings Act 1973 (ancillary and collateral orders)—

(*a*) before paragraph 3, there shall be inserted the following paragraph—

'**2A**   Any enactment or rule of law empowering a court to make an order for payment of aliment (including interim aliment).'; and

(*b*) after paragraph 12A, there shall be inserted the following paragraph—

'**12B**   Section 8 (orders for financial provision on divorce), section 17(1) (financial provision on declarator of nullity of marriage) and section 18 (orders relating to avoidance transactions) of the Family Law (Scotland) Act 1985.'

THE LAND REGISTRATION (SCOTLAND) ACT 1979 (c. 33)

10 In section 12 (3) (*b*) of the Land Registration (Scotland) Act 1979 (circumstances in which there is no entitlement to indemnity for loss), at the end there shall be added the words 'or has been set aside or varied by an order under section 18 (2) (orders relating to avoidance transactions) of the Family Law (Scotland) Act 1985'.

THE MATRIMONIAL HOMES (FAMILY PROTECTION) (SCOTLAND) ACT 1981 (c. 59)

11 For section 13 (2) of the Matrimonial Homes (Family Protection) (Scotland) Act 1981 (transfer of tenancy) there shall be substituted the following subsection—

'(2) In an action—

(*a*) for divorce, the Court of Session or a sheriff;

(*b*) for nullity of marriage, the Court of Session,

may, on granting decree or within such period as the court may specify on granting decree, make an order granting an application under subsection (1) above.'.

THE MATRIMONIAL AND FAMILY PROCEEDINGS ACT 1984 (c. 42)

12 After section 29 of the Matrimonial and Family Proceedings Act 1984 there shall be inserted the following new section—

'Application of Part IV to annulled marriages

29A This Part of this Act shall apply to an annulment, of whatever nature, of a purported marriage, as it applies to a divorce, and references to marriage and divorce shall be construed accordingly.'.

13 In section 30 (1) of that Act (interpretation of Part IV), in the definition of 'order for financial provision', for the words from 'paragraphs (*a*)' to '1976' there shall be substituted the words 'section 8 (1) of the Family Law (Scotland) Act 1985'.

Schedule 2 — Repeals

Section 28 (2)

Chapter	Short title	Extent of repeal
24 & 25 Vict. c. 86.	The Conjugal Rights (Scotland) Amendment Act 1861.	In section 6, the words from 'be held and considered' to 'as if she were unmarried, and'; the words 'the same shall'; and the words from 'provided that if any such wife' to the end of the section. In section 9, the word 'maintenance'. Sections 15 and 16.
44 & 45 Vict. c. 21.	The Married Women's Property (Scotland) Act 1881.	Sections 1 to 5. Section 8. The Schedule
10 & 11 Geo. 5. c. 54.	The Married Women's Property (Scotland) Act 1920.	The whole Act.

Chapter	Short title	Extent of repeal
15 & 16 Geo. 5. c. 45.	The Guardianship of Infants Act 1925.	Section 3 (2). In section 5 (4), the words from 'and may further order' to the end of the subsection. Section 8.
20 & 21 Geo. 5. c. 33.	The Illegitimate Children (Scotland) Act 1930.	Section 1. In section 2, in subsection (1), the words 'or in any action for aliment for an illegitimate child', and subsection (2). Section 3. Section 5.
22 & 23 Geo. 5. c. 47.	The Children and Young Persons (Scotland) Act 1932.	Section 73 (1) (*b*) and (3).
2 & 3 Geo. 6. c. 4.	The Custody of Children (Scotland) Act 1939.	In section 1, in subsection (1) the word 'maintenance' and subsection (2).
14 Geo. 6. c. 37.	The Maintenance Orders Act 1950.	Section 6 (2). In section 7, the words from 'whether' to 'maintenance of the pupil child'.
15 & 16 Geo. 6 & 1 Eliz. 2. c. 41.	The Affiliation Orders Act 1952.	The whole Act.
6 & 7 Eliz. 2. c. 40.	The Matrimonial Proceedings (Children) Act 1958.	In section 7, in subsection (1), the word 'maintenance', and subsection (2). In section 9 (1), the word 'maintenance'.
1964 c. 19.	The Married Women's Property Act 1964.	The whole Act.
1972 c. 18	The Maintenance Orders (Reciprocal Enforcement) Act 1972.	Section 31 (5).
1973 c. 45.	The Domicile and Matrimonial Proceedings Act 1973.	In Schedule 2, paragraphs 1 and 2.
1976 c. 39.	The Divorce (Scotland) Act 1976.	Sections 5 to 8.
1978 c. 22.	The Domestic Proceedings and Magistrates' Courts Act 1978.	Section 60 (1) (*a*). In Schedule 2, paragraph 1 (*a*).
1981 c. 59.	The Matrimonial Homes (Family Protection) (Scotland) Act 1981.	Section 7 (5).
1982 c. 27.	The Civil Jurisdiction and Judgments Act 1982.	In paragraph 1 of Schedule 9, the words 'for adherence and aliment or'.

Chapter	Short title	Extent of repeal
1983 c. 12.	The Divorce Jurisdiction, Court Fees and Legal Aid (Scotland) Act 1983.	In Schedule 1, paragraphs 21 and 23.
1984 c. 15.	The Law Reform (Husband and Wife) (Scotland) Act 1984.	In Schedule 1, paragraphs 3, 4 and 6.

Appendix II
Rules of Court

A. Court of Session

The Rules of Court to which amendments have been made are set out below.

Where square brackets are used, the amendment is merely summarised. In all other cases the full text of the rule, as amended, is reproduced.

SECTION 3 — CONSISTORIAL ACTIONS

Rule 154 (Application and interpretation)

[Paragraph (1) is amended so as to bring actions for financial provision after overseas divorce, and actions of aliment, within the scope of Section 3 of the Rules of Court.

Paragraph (3) provides that **'The Act of 1985'** means the Family Law (Scotland) Act 1985.]

CONCLUSIONS

Rule 156

156 (1) The form of the conclusions of the summons shall be in accordance with the appropriate form set out in Form 2.

156 (2) It shall be competent in the conclusions to include a conclusion in the following terms:— 'For such other order as the court may consider appropriate'.

Rule 160 (Intimation)

[Paragraph (1) is amended so as to substitute a reference to rule 170D (4) (*c*) and (9) for the (incorrect) reference to rule 179D (4) (*c*).]

Rule 170D

170D (1) Application by pursuer for financial provision. An application to the court under section 8(1) of the Act of 1985 by the pursuer in an action of divorce for one or more the following orders:—

   (*a*) an order for the payment of a capital sum or the transfer of property to him by the other party to the marriage;

(*b*) an order for the making of a periodical allowance to him by the other party to the marriage;

(*c*) an incidental order within the meaning of section 14(2) of the Act of 1985,

should be made by including conclusions in the terms set out in Form 2 and supporting averments in the summons specifying the nature of the order the pursuer seeks.

170D (2)   Application by defender for financial provision. An application to the Court by the defender in an action for divorce for an order mentioned in paragraph (1) shall be made in defences including in addition to supporting averments and pleas-in-law, a conclusion in the terms set out in Form 2 specifying the nature of the order the defender seeks.

170D (3)   Subsequent applications for and variation of periodical allowance. An application to the Court by either party in an action of divorce for an order under section 8 (2), by virtue of section 13 (1) (*b*) or (*c*), of the Act of 1985—

(*a*) for payment by the other party to the marriage of a periodical allowance;

(*b*) for an order for payment of periodical allowance to be varied or recalled,

shall be made by motion; and rule 170B (10) shall apply to a motion under this paragraph for an order for payment of or variation or recall of a periodical allowance, as it applies to a motion for variation or revocation of an order for aliment.

170D (4)   Applications for orders relating to avoidance transactions.

(*a*) An application to the court by either party in an action of divorce under section 18 of the Act of 1985 shall be made by including supporting conclusions, averments and pleas-in-law in the summons, defences, or minute, as the case may be.

(*b*) The applicant in an application for an order under section 18 of the Act of 1985 shall, subject to the following provisions of this paragraph, intimate the summons, defences or minute by means of which he makes that application to any third party in whose favour the transfer of, or transaction involving, property is to be or was made and to any other person having an interest in the transfer of, or transaction involving, property, and any such third party or other person may lodge answers thereto within such period as the court may allow.

(*c*) Intimation of any summons to any persons under sub-paragraph (*b*) shall be made by endorsing on the summons a warrant in the following terms: 'Warrant to intimate to (name and address) as (the person in whose favour the transfer of [*or* transaction involving] property referred to in the condescendence of this summons was made (*or* is to be made) (a person having an interest in the transfer of [*or* transaction involving] property referred to in the condescendence of this summons)'; and rule 160 shall apply to the execution of that warrant.

(*d*) Intimation of any defences or minute to any person under sub-paragraph (*b*) shall be made in accordance with an order of the court, being such order for intimation as the court thinks proper to make on the motion of the defender or minuter, as the case may be.

170D (5)   Opposition by defender to claim for financial provision or aliment. Opposition by a defender to financial provision sought by the pursuer in an action of divorce shall be made in defences.

170D (6)   Warrant for execution on decree of interim aliment pending disposal of action.

(*a*) The Principal Clerk or the Deputy Principal Clerk or anyone authorised by either of them in that behalf may append to an official certified copy of an interlocutor granting decree for interim aliment a warrant for execution in the following terms:—

'and the Lords of Council and Session grant warrant for all lawful execution upon the aforementioned decree for interim aliment.'.

(*b*) Rule 65 applies to that warrant as it applies to the warrant in an extract of a decree.

170D (7) Subsequent applications for, or variation or recall of, certain orders for financial provision. An application for an order—

    (*a*) for variation or recall under section 14 (4), of an incidental order under section 8(2), of the Act of 1985;

    (*b*) setting aside or varying an agreement as to financial provision under section 16 of the Act of 1985; or

    (*c*) relating to avoidance transactions under section 18 of the Act of 1985 after decree of divorce,

shall be made by minute in the process of the action of divorce.

170D (8) Variation of date or method of payment of capital sum or date of transfer of property. An application under section 12 (4) of the Act of 1985 shall be made by motion in the process of the action of divorce; and rule 170B (10) shall apply to a motion under this paragraph as it applies to a motion under rule 170B (10).

170D (9) Intimation to creditor. Where property, in respect of which there is an application for an order for transfer under section 8(2) of the Act of 1985, is subject to a security, there shall be intimation in Form 18E, together with a copy of the pleadings in the application, to the creditor on a warrant for intimation—

    (*a*) in the case of a summons, endorsed on the summons in the following terms:— 'Warrant to intimate to (*name and address*) as a person who is believed to be a creditor of (*name of party*); or

    (*b*) in any other case, granted by the court.

170D (10) Sisting of creditor.

    (*a*) A creditor to whom intimation has been given under paragraph (9), may apply to be heard in the cause by way of minute craving leave to be sisted as a party to the cause and making any relevant averments.

    (*b*) Where a creditor has lodged a minute under sub-paragraph (*a*), either party to the marriage may lodge answers thereto within such period as the court may allow.

170D (11) Actions of declarator of nullity of marriage. This rule applies to an action of declarator of nullity of marriage as it applies to an action of divorce.

FINANCIAL PROVISION AFTER OVERSEAS DIVORCE OR ANNULMENT

Rule 170M   Application for financial provision

170M (1) An application under section 28 or 29A of the Matrimonial and Family Proceedings Act 1984 for financial provision after a divorce or annulment in an overseas country shall be made by summons.

170M (2) An application for—

    (*a*) variation or recall of an order for periodical allowance; or

    (*b*) variation of the date or method of payment of a capital sum or the date of transfer of property under section 12 (4) of the Act of 1985,

shall be made by motion in the process of the action for financial provision under paragraph (1); and rule 170B (10) shall apply to a motion under this paragraph as it applies to a motion made under rule 170B (10).

170M (3)   An application for variation or recall of an incidental order within the meaning of section 14 (2) of the Act of 1985 shall be made by minute in the process of the action for financial provision under paragraph (1).

APPLICATIONS RELATING TO ALIMENT

Rule 170N   Undefended action of aliment

170N (1)   In an action of aliment or an application under rule 170R, rule 168 shall not apply and, subject to paragraph (2), rule 89 (decree in absence) shall apply where the defender fails to enter appearance or fails to lodge defences.

170N (2)   Where a motion for decree under paragraph (1) is enrolled, there shall be lodged all documentary evidence of the means of the parties available to the pursuer in support of the amount of aliment sought.

170N (3)   Where the court requires an appearance, the cause shall be put out for hearing as a starred motion on the Motion Roll.

Rule 170P   Variation or recall of decree of aliment

170P   An application to vary or recall a decree of aliment under section 5 of the Act of 1985 shall be made by motion in the process of the action for aliment; and rule 170B (10) shall apply to a motion made under this rule as it applies to a motion made under rule 170B (10).

Rule 170R   Variation or termination of agreement on aliment

170R   An application for variation or termination of an agreement on aliment under section 7 (2) of the Act of 1985 shall be made by summons.

FORM 18E   Rule 170D (9)

Form of intimation to a person having an interest as a creditor in the transfer of property subject to a security.

IN THE COURT OF SESSION

in causa

A B (*address*)
                              Pursuer

against

C D (*address*)

                              Defender

To (*name and address*)

TAKE NOTICE

1.   That in an action in the Court of Session, Parliament Square, Edinburgh, of which a copy of the summons [*or* defences *or* record *as the case may be*] is attached to this notice of intimation, the pursuer [*or defender*] seeks an order for the transfer of certain property to him [*or* her] under section 8 (2) of the Family Law (Scotland) Act 1985.

2.   That you may have an interest, in the property for which an order for transfer is sought, as a person having a right in security over that property being (*state property subject to the security*).

3.   That the court may not make an order under section 8 (2) of the Family Law (Scotland) Act 1985 without the consent of the creditor having a security over the property unless he has been given an opportunity of being heard by the court. Paragraph 4 of this notice of intimation informs you how you may apply to be heard by the court.

4.   That you may, if you so desire, apply to the court to be sisted as a party to the action under rule 170D (10) (*a*) of the Rules of the Court of Session in respect of your interest as a creditor, within   days after the calling of the summons which will not be earlier than
days [*or* after the expiry of   days] from the date of service of this notice of intimation. To do this you must lodge a minute in the process of the action in the Court of Session seeking leave to be sisted as a party and stating the grounds on which you wish to be heard.

Dated this   day of   19   .

                              (Signed)
                              [Solicitor for Pursuer *or* Defender],
                              (*Address*)

**YOU ARE ADVISED TO CONSULT A SOLICITOR
ABOUT THIS MATTER IMMEDIATELY.**

B.   Sheriff Court

The principal amendments to the Ordinary Cause Rules are set out below. Where the amendments are minor and consequential, they are not reproduced. Such amendments are as follows:

- all references to actions of separation and aliment are now to actions of separation;
- all references to actions of adherence and aliment are omitted;
- all references to the Mental Health (Scotland) Act 1960 are now to the Act of 1984.

Rule 3   (Initial writ)

3 (6)   Unless the sheriff on cause shown otherwise directs, in an action of divorce a warrant for citation shall not be granted without there being produced with the initial writ—

(*a*)   an extract of the relevant entry in the register of marriages; and

(*b*)   where appropriate, an extract of the relevant entry in the register of births.

Rule 11   (Citation of persons whose address is unknown)

11 (1)   Without prejudice to the provisions of rule 11A, where a defender's address is unknown to the pursuer, the sheriff shall grant warrant to cite the defender—

(*a*)   by the publication in a newspaper circulating in the area of the defender's last known address of an advertisement as nearly as may be in accordance with Form E as set out in the Appendix to this Schedule; or

(*b*)   by displaying on the walls of court a copy of the instance and crave of the initial writ, warrant of citation and notice as nearly as may be in accordance with Form E1 as set out in the Appendix to this Schedule,

and the period of notice, which shall be fixed by the sheriff, shall run from the date of publication of the advertisement or display on the walls of court, as the case may be.

11 (2)   Where citation requires to be effected under paragraph (1), the pursuer shall lodge a service copy of the initial writ and a copy of the warrant of citation with the sheriff clerk from whom they may be uplifted by the defender.

11 (5)   Where display on the walls of court is required under paragraph (1) (*b*), the pursuer shall supply to the sheriff clerk for that purpose a certified copy of the instance and crave of the initial writ and the warrant of citation.

Rule 11A   (Intimation in certain actions of divorce or separation)

11A (3)   Intimation to a person mentioned in sub-paragraphs (*a*) to (*c*) of paragraph (1) shall be as nearly as may be in accordance with Form V1 (where the defender is suffering from mental disorder) or Form V2 (where the defender's address is unknown) as set out in the Appendix to this Schedule.

11A (6)   A person receiving intimation under paragraph (1) may apply within the period of notice by minute craving to be sisted as a party and for leave to lodge defences or answers as the case may be.

Rule 34   Minute relating to aliment, periodical allowance, capital payment or transfer of property

34 (1)   In an action of separation, affiliation and aliment or for custody of a child, a defender who intends only to dispute the amount of aliment may, in place of lodging a notice of intention to defend, lodge a minute to that effect condescending on the relevant facts.

34 (2) In an action of divorce, a defender who intends only to dispute liability for, or the amount of, or raise other matters relating to, aliment, periodical allowance, capital payment or transfer of property may, in place of lodging a notice of intention to defend, lodge a minute condescending on the relevant facts.

34 (3) In an action of divorce or of separation, a defender may, without lodging a notice of intention to defend, apply to the court by minute craving an order for aliment, periodical allowance, capital payment or transfer of property and such minute shall crave the order which he claims the sheriff should make, and condescend on the relevant facts.

34 (4) On the lodging of a minute under paragraph (1), (2) or (3)—

(*a*) the sheriff clerk shall enrol the cause for a hearing, and the defender shall send a copy of the minute and intimate the date of the hearing to the pursuer; and

(*b*) the pursuer shall return the initial writ to the sheriff clerk at or before the hearing, but shall not, unless the sheriff otherwise directs, require to lodge a process.

34 (5) At the hearing, the sheriff may resolve the matter or continue the cause for such further procedure as he considers appropriate.

34 (6) In an action referred to in this rule, the sheriff may grant decree in terms of a joint minute dealing with aliment, periodical allowance, capital payment or transfer of property whether or not these have been craved in the initial writ or minute.

Rule 56 (Counter-claim for custody, access or maintenance)

56 (1) In any case in which custody of, access to, or maintenance for, a child is sought or could competently be sought the defender may make any claim relating to such matters of a kind which a pursuer may make in such a cause; and rules 51 to 55 shall apply to any such claim as they apply to a counter-claim.

56 (2) Where a defender makes a counter-claim under paragraph (1), he may, where it would otherwise be competent, incorporate a crave for an order for aliment, periodical allowance, capital payment or transfer of property rather than proceed by way of separate minute under rule 34.

56 (3) In a cause referred to in this rule, the sheriff may grant decree in terms of a joint minute dealing with custody of, access to, or maintenance for, a child, aliment, periodical allowance, capital payment or transfer of property whether or not those have been craved in the initial writ or counter-claim.

Rule 59A Late appearance by defender in actions of divorce and of separation

59A (1) The sheriff may make an order, with or without conditions, allowing a defender in an action of divorce or of separation who has not lodged a notice of intention to defend or defences—

(*a*) to appear and be heard at a diet of proof:

(*b*) to lodge defences and to lead evidence at any time before decree of divorce or of separation has been pronounced; or

(*c*) to appeal within 14 days of the decree of divorce or of separation.

59A (2) Where an order is made under paragraph (1) (*a*), a defender may not lead evidence without the consent of the pursuer.

59A (3) Where an order is made under paragraph (1) (*b*), the pursuer may lead further evidence, by recalling witnesses already examined or otherwise, whether or not he closed his proof before the order was made.

Rule 129   Recall or variation of decrees for aliment or orders for financial provision and of decrees regarding the custody of and access to children

129 (1)   Subject to paragraph (4), applications to which paragraph (2) applies shall be made by minute lodged in the original process in which decree was pronounced or an order granted.

129 (2)   This rule applies to applications for—

(*a*) the recall or variation of a sheriff court decree for payment of aliment whether pronounced in favour of a spouse, a parent, or any other person or pronounced in respect of a legitimate or illegitimate child; or

(*b*) recall or variation of a periodical allowance;

(*c*) variation of the date or method of payment of a capital sum;

(*d*) variation of the date of transfer of property;

(*e*) the recall or variation of any decree regulating the custody of or access to legitimate or illegitimate children; or

(*f*) the recall or variation of an incidental order as defined in section 14 (2) of the Family Law (Scotland) Act 1985 made before, on, or after, the date of the decree of divorce.

129 (3)   The sheriff shall order the minute to be served on any other party and appoint answers to be lodged within a specified time and shall thereafter without closing the record, and after such proof or other procedure as to the sheriff seems necessary, dispose of the application.

129 (4)   In an action of divorce or of separation, a party may, without making application under paragraph (1), crave an order relating to custody, aliment of or access to the children of the marriage, or aliment of one of the parties, notwithstanding that an order to the same or different effect has been made in a previous sheriff court process whether in the same or another sheriff court and the sheriff may make such new order thereanent as the circumstances at the date of the order require, whereupon the previous order shall cease to apply.

Rule 130   Intimation

130 (1) (*a*)   In an action where—

(i) adultery is averred by the pursuer or defender;

(ii) the name of the person with whom adultery is alleged to have been committed is disclosed in the action; and

(iii) such person is not a party to the action,

the sheriff shall not allow inquiry until a copy of the initial writ and a form of intimation as nearly as may be in accordance with Form H1 as set out in the Appendix to this Schedule have been intimated to such person or until the sheriff is satisfied that the address of such person is unknown.

(*b*) An order for such intimation may be contained in the original warrant of citation or intimation may be appointed to be made at a later stage.

(*c*) The requirement to intimate under this paragraph shall not apply where the pursuer alleges rape upon, or incest with, a named person by the defender.

130 (2) (*a*)   In an action in which the pursuer alleges sodomy or any homosexual relationship between the defender and a named person, the pursuer shall, immediately after the expiry of the period of notice, enrol a motion for intimation to that person, and the sheriff, at the hearing of the motion, may make such order for intimation or for dispensing with intimation to that person as seems just.

(*b*) Where intimation is ordered under this paragraph, a form of intimation as nearly as may be in accordance with Form H2 as set out in the Appendix to this Schedule and a copy of the initial writ shall be intimated to the named person.

130 (3)   Where the sheriff makes an order dispensing with intimation under paragraph (2), he may also make an order that the name of that person be deleted from the condescendence in the initial writ.

130 (4)   In an action in which the sheriff may make an order in respect of the custody of a child—

(*a*)   who is in the care of a local authority; or

(*b*)   who is a child of one spouse (including an illegitimate or an adopted child), being a child under the age of 16 years and who is liable to be maintained by a third party,

the pursuer shall intimate a copy of the initial writ and form of intimation as nearly as may be in accordance with Form H3 as set out in the Appendix to this Schedule to the local authority or third party concerned.

130 (5)   In an action relating to a marriage which was entered into under a law which permits polygamy and in which a decree of separation or a decree of divorce is sought, and either party to the marriage in question has any spouse additional to the other party, the warrant of citation shall include an order for intimation of the action to such additional spouse and the pursuer shall intimate a copy of the initial writ and form of intimation as nearly as may be in accordance with Form H4 as set out in the Appendix to this Schedule to such additional spouse.

130 (6)   In an action in which the sheriff may make an order in respect of the custody of a child who is in *de facto* custody of a third party, the pursuer shall intimate a copy of the initial writ and form of intimation as nearly as may be in accordance with Form H5 as set out in the Appendix to this Schedule to the third party concerned.

130 (7)   In an action in which the sheriff—

(*a*)   proposes to commit the care of a child to an individual other than one of the parties to the marriage or to a local authority under section 10 of the Matrimonial Proceedings (Children) Act 1958 or section 11 (1) (*a*) of the Guardianship Act 1973; the pursuer shall intimate a copy of the initial writ and form of intimation as nearly as may be in accordance with Form H6 as set out in the Appendix to this Schedule to the individual or local authority concerned; or

(*b*)   has made an order placing a child under the supervision of a local authority under section 12 of the Matrimonial Proceedings (Children) Act 1958 or section 11 (1) (*b*) of the Guardianship Act 1973; the sheriff clerk shall send a form of intimation thereof as nearly as may be in accordance with Form H6A as set out in the Appendix to this Schedule to the local authority concerned.

130 (8)   In an action for custody of a child by a person by virtue of section 47 (1) of the Children Act 1975, that person shall give notice to—

(*a*)   the local authority within whose area that person resides within seven days of lodging the action; or

(*b*)   in any other case, such local authority as the court may direct under section 49 (1) of the Children Act 1975,

by intimating to the local authority a copy of the initial writ together with a notice as nearly as may be in accordance with Form T2 as set out in the Appendix to this Schedule.

130 (9)   In an action in which an order is sought by a pursuer or defender under section 8 (1) of the Family Law (Scotland) Act 1985 for the transfer of property subject to security in which the consent of the creditor has not been obtained, the party seeking the order shall intimate a copy of the initial writ and form of intimation as nearly as may be in accordance with Form H7 as set out in the Appendix to this Schedule, to the creditor.

130 (10)   Intimation under paragraph (4) or (5) may be dispensed with if the sheriff is satisfied that the address of the person to whom intimation is to be made is unknown.

130 (11) (*a*) Intimation under this rule shall be on a period of notice of fourteen days unless the sheriff shall consider it appropriate in the circumstances to appoint another period; provided that in no circumstances shall the period of notice be less than forty eight hours.

(*b*) All warrants for intimation except those under paragraph (2), or where the period of notice is varied, may be signed by the sheriff clerk in conjunction with a warrant of citation under rule 8 (1).

130 (12) A person receiving intimation under paragraph (1), (2), (4), (5), (6), (7)(*a*) or (9) may apply within the period of notice by minute craving to be sisted as a party and for leave to lodge defences or answers as the case may be.

130 (13) (*a*) A minute lodged under paragraph (12) shall be accompanied by the service copy of the intimation.

(*b*) On receiving such a minute, the sheriff clerk shall assign a diet in the cause for a date after the expiry of the period of notice and the sheriff shall, at the diet, regulate the further procedure in the cause.

(*c*) The sheriff may authorise proof by affidavit evidence in respect of any matter not in dispute between the parties.

Rule 132A Applications under the Family Law (Scotland) Act 1985

132A (1) Where, in an action in which an alimentary crave is or may be made, a party seeks an order under section 7 (2) of the Family Law (Scotland) Act 1985 ('the 1985 Act') (variation or termination of agreement on aliment) he shall do so either in the initial writ or by separate minute in the process.

132A (2) Where an order referred to in paragraph (1) is sought in any other circumstances, application for the order shall be by way of summary application.

132A (3) Where a party seeks an order under section 16 (1) (*a*) of the 1985 Act (order setting aside or varying term of agreement relating to a periodical allowance), application for the order shall be by way of summary application.

132A (4) Where a party in an action of divorce seeks an order under section 16 (1) (*b*) of the 1985 Act (agreement or financial provision not fair and reasonable), he shall do so either in the initial writ or by separate minute in the process or, if appropriate, by way of counter-claim.

Rule 138 (Citation in simplified divorce procedure)

138 (9) Where, in an application, the facts in section 1 (2) (*e*) of the Act of 1976 are relied on and the address of the respondent is unknown—

(*a*) citation of the respondent shall be effected by displaying a copy of the application and notice as nearly as may be in accordance with Form SDA6 as set out in the Appendix to this Schedule on the walls of court and the period of notice shall be fourteen days; and

(*b*) intimation shall be made to—

(i) every child of the marriage between the parties; and

(ii) one of the next of kin of the respondent who has reached the age of 12 years in the case of a girl and 14 years in the case of a boy.

138 (10) Intimation to a person referred to in sub-paragraph 9 (*b*) (i) and (ii) shall be effected by intimating a copy of the application and form of intimation as nearly as may be in accordance with Form SDA7 as set out in the Appendix to this Schedule.

138 (11) Intimation to a person referred to in sub-paragraph 9 (*b*) (i) and (ii) shall not be required under paragraph 10 if the address of that person is unknown to the applicant.

Rule 142   Appeal in simplified divorce procedure

142 A respondent may, within 14 days of the date of an interlocutor granting decree of divorce, appeal against that interlocutor by addressing a letter to the court giving reasons for his appeal.

Existing forms

Certain minor amendments are made to existing forms. These are as follows:

(*a*) in Form D, after the words 'with me subscribing', insert the words 'in actions of divorce and separation also set forth any forms sent in accordance with rule 131';

(*b*) in Form E, for the words 'he should immediately contact the sheriff clerk (address)' substitute the words 'or to make any claim therein he/she should immediately contact the sheriff clerk (address) from whom he/she may obtain the service copy initial writ.';

(*c*) in Form P, for the words 'rule 141' substitute the words 'rule 128'; and for the words 'rule 141 (2)', substitute the words 'rule 128 (2)';

(*d*) in Form S in the heading, omit the words 'and aliment';

(*e*) in Form S2 in the heading, omit the words 'and aliment';

(*f*) in Form T—

   (*a*) omit the words 'and aliment' wherever they occur;

   (*b*) omit the words '(signed) witness';

(*g*) in Form T2 for the words 'rule 130 (9)' substitute the words 'rule 130 (8)'; and

(*h*) in form V omit the words 'and aliment'.

New forms

FORM E1   Rule 11 (1) (*b*)

DISPLAY ON THE WALLS OF COURT

Court Ref No.

An Action has been raised in   Sheriff Court by A.B. pursuer
calling as a defender C.D. whose last known address was

If C.D. wishes to defend the action or to make any claim therein he/she should immediately contact the Sheriff Clerk (*address*) from whom he/she may obtain the service copy Initial Writ.

Tel No:

(*Signed*) Sheriff Clerk
Date: (*insert date*)

Family Law (Scotland) Act 1985

           Rule 130 (1) (*a*)

FORM OF INTIMATION TO ALLEGED ADULTERER IN ACTION OF DIVORCE OR SEPARATION

To (*name and address as in the Warrant*)

Take note that in an action number (*'A' number*), you are alleged to have committed adultery. A copy of the Initial Writ is attached. If you wish to dispute the truth of the allegation made against you, you may lodge a minute with the Sheriff Clerk (*insert full address of Sheriff Clerk*) for leave to appear as a party. Your minute must be lodged within [14] days from (*insert date*), the date of posting of this intimation.

Date: (*insert date*)   (*Signed*) A.B.
                                           [Solicitor for Pursuer]

NOTE

The minute to be lodged with the Sheriff Clerk must be in proper form. You should crave to be sisted as a party to the action and seek leave to lodge defences or answers. The minute must be accompanied by the appropriate fee of (£   ).

It may be in your best interests to consult a solicitor who, if necessary, will advise you on the availability of legal aid.

           Rule 130 (2) (*b*)

FORM OF INTIMATION TO PERSON WITH WHOM AN IMPROPER ASSOCIATION IS ALLEGED TO HAVE OCCURRED

To (*name and address as in the Warrant*)

Take note that in an action number (*'A' number*), the defender is alleged to have had an improper association with you. A copy of the Initial Writ is attached. If you wish to dispute the truth of the allegation made against you, you may lodge a minute with the Sheriff Clerk (*insert full address of Sheriff Clerk*) for leave to appear as a party. Your minute must be lodged within [14] days from (*insert date*), the date of posting of this intimation.

Date: (*insert date*)   (*Signed*) A.B.
                                           [Solicitor for Pursuer]

NOTE

The minute to be lodged with the Sheriff Clerk must be in proper form. You should crave to be sisted as a party to the action and seek leave to lodge defences or answers. The minute must be accompanied by the appropriate fee of (£   ).

It may be in your best interests to consult a solicitor who, if necessary, will advise you on the availability of legal aid.

FORM H3   Rule 130 (4)

FORM OF INTIMATION TO A LOCAL AUTHORITY OR THIRD PARTY WHO MAY BE LIABLE TO MAINTAIN A CHILD

To (*name and address as in the Warrant*)

Take note that in an action number (*'A' number*), the Court may make an order in respect of the custody of (*name and address*) a child in your care [*or* liable to be maintained by you]. A copy of the Initial Writ is attached. If you wish to appear as a party, you may lodge a minute with the Sheriff Clerk (*inset full address of Sheriff Clerk*), for leave to do so. Your minute must be lodged within [14] days from (*insert date*), the date of posting of this intimation.

Date: (*insert date*)   (*Signed*) A.B.
                                             [Solicitor for Pursuer]

NOTE

The minute to be lodged with the Sheriff Clerk must be in proper form. You should crave to be sisted as a party to the action and seek leave to lodge defences or answers. The minute must be accompanied by the appropriate fee of (£   ).

It may be in your best interests to consult a solicitor who, if necessary, will advise you on the availability of legal aid.

FORM H4   Rule 130 (5)

FORM OF INTIMATION TO ADDITIONAL SPOUSE OF EITHER PARTY IN PROCEEDINGS RELATING TO A POLYGAMOUS MARRIAGE

To (*name and address as in the Warrant*)

Take note that an action for divorce [*or* separation] number (*'A' number*), involves (*name and designation*) your spouse. A copy of the Initial Writ is attached. If you wish to appear as a party, you may lodge a minute with the Sheriff Clerk (*insert full address of Sheriff Clerk*), for leave to do so. Your minute must be lodged within [14] days from (*insert date*), the date of posting of this intimation.

Date: (*insert date*)   (*Signed*) A.B.
                                             [Solicitor for Pursuer]

NOTE

The minute to be lodged with the Sheriff Clerk must be in proper form. You should crave to be sisted as a party to the action and seek leave to lodge defences or answers. The minute must be accompanied by the appropriate fee of (£   ).

It may be in your best interests to consult a solicitor who, if necessary, will advise you on the availability of legal aid.

Family Law (Scotland) Act 1985

FORM H5   Rule 130 (6)

FORM OF INTIMATION TO PERSON HAVING *DE FACTO* CUSTODY OF CHILDREN

To (*name and address as in the Warrant*)

Take note that in an action number (*'A' number*), the court may make an order in respect of the custody of (*name and address*) a child/children at present in your custody. A copy of the Initial Writ is attached. If you wish to appear as a party, you may lodge a minute with the Sheriff Clerk (*insert full address of Sheriff Clerk*), for leave to do so. Your minute must be lodged within [14] days from (*insert date*), the date of posting of this intimation.

Date: (*insert date*)   (*Signed*) A.B.
                                            [Solicitor for Pursuer]

NOTE

The minute to be lodged with the Sheriff Clerk must be in proper form. You should crave to be sisted as a party to the action and seek leave to lodge defences or answers. The minute must be accompanied by the appropriate fee of (£   ).

It may be in your best interests to consult a solicitor who, if necessary, will advise you on the availability of legal aid.

FORM H6   Rule 130 (7) (*a*)

FORM OF INTIMATION TO LOCAL AUTHORITY OR THIRD PARTY TO WHOM CARE OF A CHILD IS TO BE GIVEN

To (*name and address as in the Warrant*)

Take note that in an action number (*'A' number*), the court proposes to commit to your care the child (*name and address*). A copy of the Initial Writ is attached. If you wish to appear as a party, you may lodge a minute with the Sheriff Clerk (*insert full address of Sheriff Clerk*), for leave to do so. Your minute must be lodged within [14] days from (*insert date*), the date of posting of this intimation.

Date: (*insert date*)   (*Signed*) A.B.
                                            [Solicitor for Pursuer]

NOTE

The minute to be lodged with the Sheriff Clerk must be in proper form. You should crave to be sisted as a party to the action and seek leave to lodge defences or answers. The minute must be accompanied by the appropriate fee of (£   ).

It may be in your best interests to consult a solicitor who, if necessary, will advise you on the availability of legal aid.

FORM H6A   Rule 130 (7) (*b*)

FORM OF INTIMATION TO LOCAL AUTHORITY OF SUPERVISION ORDER

Initial Writ

in

A.B. (*Address*)   Pursuer(s)

against

C.D. (*Address*)   Defender(s)

To (*name and address of local authority*)

TAKE NOTICE

That on (*date*) in the Sheriff Court at (*place*) the Sheriff made a supervision order under *section 12 of the Matrimonial Proceedings (Children) Act 1958/* section 11 (1) (*b*) of the Guardianship Act 1973, placing the child (*name and address*) under your supervision. A certified copy of the sheriff's interlocutor is attached hereto.

Date: (*insert date*)   (*Signed*) A.B.
                                                  Sheriff Clerk

*Delete as appropriate

FORM H7

Rule 130 (9)

FORM OF INTIMATION TO CREDITOR IN APPLICATION FOR ORDER FOR THE TRANSFER OF PROPERTY UNDER SECTION 8 OF THE FAMILY LAW (SCOTLAND) ACT 1985

To (*name and address as in the Warrant*)

Take note that in an action number ('*A*' *number*) an order is sought for the transfer of property (*specify the order*), over which you hold a security. A copy of the Initial Writ is attached. If you wish to appear as a party, you may lodge a minute with the Sheriff Clerk (*insert full address of Sheriff Clerk*), for leave to do so. Your minute must be lodged within [14] days from (*insert date*), the date of posting of this intimation.

Date: (*insert date*)   (*Signed*) A.B.
                                                  [Solicitor for Pursuer]

NOTE

The minute to be lodged with the Sheriff Clerk must be in proper form. You should crave to be sisted as a party to the action and seek leave to lodge defences or answers. The minute must be accompanied by the appropriate fee of (£   ).
It may be in your best interests to consult a solicitor who, if necessary, will advise you on the availability of legal aid.

Family Law (Scotland) Act 1985

FORM V1   Rule 11A (3)

FORM OF INTIMATION TO CHILDREN, NEXT OF KIN AND *CURATOR BONIS* IN AN ACTION OF DIVORCE OR SEPARATION WHERE THE DEFENDER SUFFERS FROM A MENTAL DISORDER

To (*name and address as in the Warrant*)

Take note that an action of divorce [*or* separation] number (*'A' number*) has been raised against (*name, and designation*) your (father, mother, brother or other relative, or ward, as the case may be). A copy of the Initial Writ is attached. If you wish to appear as a party, you may lodge a minute with the Sheriff Clerk (*insert full address of Sheriff Clerk*), for leave to do so. Your minute must be lodged within [14] days from (*insert date*), the date of posting of this intimation.

Date: (*insert date*)   (*Signed*) A.B.
                                                 [Solicitor for Pursuer]

NOTE

The minute to be lodged with the Sheriff Clerk must be in proper form. You should crave to be sisted as a party to the action and seek leave to lodge defences or answers. The minute must be accompanied by the appropriate fee of (£   ).

It may be in your best interests to consult a solicitor who, if necessary, will advise you on the availability of legal aid.

FORM V2

Rule 11A (3)

FORM OF INTIMATION TO CHILDREN AND NEXT OF KIN IN AN ACTION OF DIVORCE OR SEPARATION WHERE THE DEFENDER'S ADDRESS IS UNKNOWN

To (*name and address as in the Warrant*)

Take note that an action of divorce [*or* separation] number (*'A' number*), has been raised against (*name*) your [father, mother, brother or other relative *as the case may be*]. If you know of his/her present address, you are requested to forward the same to the Sheriff Clerk (*insert full address of Sheriff Clerk*) forthwith. You may also if you wish to appear as a party lodge a minute with the Sheriff Clerk for leave to do so. Your minute must be lodged within [14] days from (*insert date*), the date of posting of this intimation.

Date: (*insert date*)   (*Signed*) A.B.
                                                 [Solicitor for Pursuer]

NOTE

The minute to be lodged with the Sheriff Clerk must be in proper form. You should crave to be sisted as a party to the action and seek leave to lodge defences or answers. The minute must be accompanied by the appropriate fee of (£   ).
It may be in your best interests to consult a solicitor who, if necessary, will advise you on the availability of legal aid.

FORM SDA6   Rule 138 (9)

FORM OF INTIMATION FOR DISPLAY ON WALLS OF COURT

Court Ref. No:

An application for divorce has been made in   Sheriff Court by
A.B. calling as defender C.D.

If C.D. wishes to oppose the granting of decree of divorce he/she should immediately contact the Sheriff Clerk from whom he/she may obtain a copy of the application.

Tel No:—

Date: (insert date)   (*Signed*)   Sheriff Clerk

FORM SDA7

Rule 138 (10)

FORM OF INTIMATION TO CHILDREN AND NEXT OF KIN IN SIMPLIFIED DIVORCE APPLICATION

To (*name and address*)

TAKE NOTICE that an application for divorce (*number of application*) has been made against (*name of respondent*) your [father, mother, brother or other relative *as the case may be*]. A copy of the application is attached. If you know of his/her present address, you are requested to forward it to the Sheriff Clerk (*insert full address of Sheriff Clerk*) forthwith. You may also, if you wish, oppose the granting of decree of divorce by sending a letter to the court giving your reasons for your opposition to the application. Your letter must be sent to the Sheriff Clerk within [14] days from (*insert date*), the date of posting of this intimation.

Date: (*insert date*)   (*Signed*)   A.B.
                                             Sheriff Clerk

NOTE

It may be in your best interests to consult a solicitor, who if necessary, will advise you on the availability of legal aid.

Appendix III

Examples of Awards of Financial Provision Under the New Principles

Introduction

The examples given in this Appendix of awards of financial provision under the principles discussed in Chapter 4 are not intended to be comprehensive. They represent rather an attempt to illustrate some of the commoner situations which will arise in practice. Each example relates to a particular principle rather than to a combination of principles; the latter will, of course, often be encountered in practice. No attempt has been made to devise complex examples or to provide detailed mathematical calculations (taking into account, for instance, the effect of inflation, or tax implications). In many areas, as where property is used for business purposes, existing case law will provide appropriate illustrations. Inevitably some of the observations made are more conjectural than others. All persons are fictitious.

Meaning of Matrimonial Property

Example 1 (ss. 9 (1) (a), 10)

The title to Mr and Mrs Adder's house is in Mr Adder's name. The house was bought shortly after the marriage. He alone has been repaying the building society loan. His wife claims a half share in the net proceeds of the house. Mr Adder responds that she should receive only one third, because that has always been the appropriate norm, and in any event she did not make any financial contribution. Mrs Adder counters that, whatever may have been the previous custom, it is no longer sound law; it is immaterial that she has not been earning and that he has made the repayments; the property has been acquired by the joint efforts of the parties. The court awards her a half share.

Family Law (Scotland) Act 1985

Example 2 (ss. 9 (1) (a), 10)

The title to Mr and Mrs Badger's house is in joint names. The house was purchased five years ago, shortly after the marriage, for £40,000. Half of the purchase price was provided by a building society, and half came from the net proceeds of the sale of Mr Badger's bachelor flat. The house is worth £70,000 at the date of separation. Mrs Badger claims a half share in the net proceeds, i.e. £25,000. Mr Badger contends that £20,000 (representing the proceeds of sale of his flat) should be deducted, and that his wife's share should be £15,000. He considers he has enough evidence to satisfy the sheriff of the source of the funds.

Example 3 (ss. 9 (1), (a), 10, 11 (7))

The title to Mr and Mrs Coney's house is in joint names. The house was purchased shortly after the marriage. Mr Coney claims that, in addition to carrying out her normal household duties, Mrs Coney used to entertain gentlemen friends, in the back parlour, for a consideration. In divorce proceedings, he claims that her share in the net proceeds of the house should be reduced on account of her misconduct. She points out that her conduct is not relevant in the assessment of her share, because it has not affected the economic basis of her claim (s. 11 (7) (a)). She concedes, however, that the profits which she has garnered from her extramarital activities form part of the matrimonial property.

Example 4 (ss. 9 (1) (a), 10)

The title to Mr and Mrs Dog's flat is in her name alone. This is because they used to live with her aged mother, who left her house to her daughter. The present flat was bought by Mrs Dog out of the proceeds of sale. Mr Dog's claim for a half share in the value of the flat is rejected, because the flat is not part of the matrimonial property.

Example 5 (ss. 9 (1) (a), 10)

Mr Emu is a forty five year old civil servant. Part of his salary is deducted at source for superannuation. By the time he retires at sixty he will have worked as a civil servant for thirty seven years. This figure will determine his pension entitlement. Mrs Emu claims that the value of his rights on retirement should be included in the matrimonial property. Mr Emu points out that they have only been married for ten years and that only the proportion of his eventual entitlement representing those ten years should be included. In order to reach a settlement the parties agree to be bound by a valuation made by an actuary.

Example 6 (ss. 8, 9 (1) (a), 10)

Mr Fox is quite well-off. In addition to the matrimonial home in Edinburgh, he has a Highland estate which belonged to his father (and which is therefore not matrimonial property). Mrs

Fox's overall claim for financial provision contains a conclusion for the transfer to her of the Highland estate but not of the house in Edinburgh. The court is not precluded from transferring the estate in full or partial settlement of her claim.

Example 7 (ss. 9 (1) (*a*), 10)

Mr Gnu is an indigent teacher. After the Gnus separate, he gives up teaching and starts a successful education advisory service. Mrs Gnu's claim includes part of the value of the business. This is rejected, because the business is not part of the matrimonial property.

Economic Advantages and Disadvantages

Example 8 (ss. 9 (1) (*b*), 11 (2), (7), 13 (2))

Mr Hogg is a Q.C. aged fifty five. He has few assets, but a reasonably good income. His wife, who is forty five, married him as soon as she obtained a First Class honours degree from Oxford and has never worked. After the separation she obtained employment as a secretary. If she had worked throughout the marriage she might have been earning £10,000 pa more. There is insufficient matrimonial property to compensate her for any loss. One way of valuing her claim is to take a figure representing the annual difference in earning capacity, and to apply an appropriate multiplicand having regard to her age and to the number of years she is likely to be earning. An award might take the form of a lump sum, payable in instalments which Mr Hogg can make from his earnings. The court cannot make an order for periodical allowance (s. 13 (2)). (Mrs Hogg may also claim under s. 9 (1) (*e*) – see Example 12.) Mr Hogg also alleges that the marriage broke down because of Mrs Hogg's desertion, but the court refuses to take this into account (s. 11 (7)).

Example 9 (ss. 9 (1) (*b*), 11 (2) (*b*))

As in Example 8; but there is substantial matrimonial property. In the course of the hearing it is suggested to the sheriff that if Mrs Hogg receives half of the matrimonial property, and is also given sole occupation of the matrimonial home and sole use of the furniture etc., her claim will be adequately satisfied. (Again, Mrs Hogg may also claim under s. 9 (1) (*e*) – see Example 12.)

Economic Burden of Child Care

Example 10 (ss. 9 (1) (*c*), 11 (3), (7))

Mr and Mrs Joey have three children aged nine, seven and five. Mrs Joey has secretarial qualifications, but is reluctant to work until the youngest child is sixteen. Her husband is prepared to agree that she should not work for a few years, but thinks that a periodical allowance for eleven years is too long: he suggests that an award should initially be for five years, and that his wife should apply for a fresh order at the end of that period if the circumstances so warrant. The material effect of his suggestion is that Mrs Joey, rather than Mr Joey, would have to take the initiative in having the financial position reassessed. He also contends that the amount of the claim should be reduced because she habitually attacked him with a broom-handle when he returned from the pub; the court, however, refuse to take this into account (s. 11 (7)).

The Three-Year Adjustment Period

Example 11 (ss. 9 (1) (*d*), 11 (4), (7))

Mr and Mrs Koala separate after five years' marriage. Mrs Koala is in her mid-twenties, has no children, and has not worked during the marriage. She is intelligent and would like to spend, say, four years reading for an honours degree at Edinburgh, followed by a year's post-graduate research at Aix-en-Provence, followed by two or three years' further research, preferably in the United States. There is little matrimonial property of any value and she therefore claims a periodical allowance. The court is prepared in principle to make an award, but only for three years, on the view that she cannot establish serious financial hardship (s. 9 (1) (*e*)). Mr Koala then says his wife walked out on him without cause, and that in the circumstances it is unreasonable he should have to pay anything. The court has power to take this form of conduct into account (s. 11 (7) (*b*)).

Serious Financial Hardship

Example 12 (ss. 9 (1) (*e*), 11 (5), (7))

Mr and Mrs Leo are both aged fifty five. There is little matrimonial property, but Mr Leo will have a good pension when he retires at sixty. Mrs Leo has no qualifications and has been unable, at the time of the divorce, to obtain employment of any kind. She asks the court to award her a periodical allowance without a definite time-limit (i.e. until her death or remarriage). Mr Leo wants the order to be limited to five years, as his income will be reduced when he is sixty. Depending on all the circumstances the court may accede to either suggestion. The material effect of Mr Leo's suggestion is that Mrs Leo would have to take the initiative in having the financial position reassessed. Mr Leo also says that his wife frequently consorted with other men, and that this was the cause of marital breakdown. The court has power to take this form of conduct into account (s. 11 (7) (*b*)).

Case Table

Family Law (Scotland) Act 1985

Legislation Finding List

Index